£ 2

KU-247-844

The Marrying Kind

Brenda Maddox

The Marrying Kind

Homosexuality and Marriage

GRANADA
London Toronto Sydney New York

Granada Publishing Limited
Frogmore, St Albans, Herts AL2 2NF
and
36 Golden Square, London W1R 4AH
866 United Nations Plaza, New York, NY 10017, USA
117 York Street, Sydney, NSW 2000, Australia
100 Skyway Avenue, Rexdale, Ontario M9W 3A6, Canada
61 Beach Road, Auckland, New Zealand

Published by Granada Publishing 1982

Copyright © Brenda Maddox 1982

British Library Cataloguing in Publication Data

Maddox, Brenda
   The marrying kind: homosexuality and
   marriage.
   1. Marriage
   2. Homosexuals—Attitudes
   I. Title
   306.8   HQ734

ISBN 0–246–11189–5

Printed in Great Britain by
Richard Clay (The Chaucer Press) Ltd, Bungay, Suffolk

All rights reserved. No part of this publication may be
reproduced, stored in a retrieval system, or transmitted,
in any form or by any means, electronic, mechanical,
photocopying, recording or otherwise, without the prior
permission of the publishers.

Granada ®
Granada Publishing ®

Contents

. . . dozing beneath a coverlet of newspapers in the den, the fire crackling beside him, the house filled with the faraway shouts of children playing in rooms upstairs, of adults playing cards in the dining room, he looked up once at the dog – and the dog looked up, inquiring, at him. 'I'm gay', he whispered to the dog. The snow was falling lightly through the delicate branches of the fir trees pressed against the windowpanes, and he thought of it falling on all the shopping centers in the hills around that town, filled with families just like this one, and he heard the hiss of station wagons passing on the road outside, filled with children in Eskimo hoods, dozing in each other's laps. He smiled at the quirk of fate that kept him from it all like a prisoner being escorted down the corridor of a hospital in handcuffs, past the other patients, and then he fell asleep.

Dancer from the Dance by Andrew Holleran

Acknowledgements

My book has been made possible primarily by the kindness and trust of those whom I cannot thank by name. I am also grateful for the help of many others who made suggestions on content or style or who answered my questions about history, law, psychiatry, religion and social attitudes. Among those to whom I am indebted are:

Barbara Bagenal, Catherine S. Baker, Professor Charles R. Beye, Dr John Birchnall, Dr Lee Birk, The Rt Rev Msgnr Ralph Brown, the Rev Dudley Cave, the late Nicholas Davenport, Wallace Dickson, Delia Doherty, the Rev Jim N. Dykes, Penny and Ray Edwards, John and Theresa Finney, Jackie Forster, Doris Jonas Freed, Dr M. Glasser, Paul C. Glick, Anthony Grey, Mr and Mrs Peter Grose, Dr Lawrence J. and Dr Myra S. Hatterer, Michael Holroyd, Maureen Howard, Roland Jeffrey, Dr Thomas Kelly, the Rev Richard Kirker, Andrew Knight, Ann Lapping, Dr Muriel Laskin, Denis Lemon, Diarmaid MacCulloch, John J. McNeill, John, Bronwen and Bruno Maddox, Dr Richard Pillard, Chaim Raphael, Susan Raven, Lord Rossins, Nora Sayre, Maura Shaw, Robert Skidelsky, Jeanne Solomon, Michael Steed, Michael Wall, Allen Weinstein, the Rev Robert Wheatly and Dr Norman Zinberg.

I should also like to express my thanks to the following: American Civil Liberties Union, Boston Homophile Community Center, Campaign for Homosexual Equality, Families Need Fathers, Gay Christian Movement, *Gay Community News*, Gay Daddies, *Gay News*, London Friend, London Library, National Gay Task Force, National Institute of Mental Health, members of the New York Police Department, 6th Precinct, Portman Clinic, Sappho, Sigma and the Tavistock Institute.

The author wishes to thank the following for permission to quote from the works listed: The Hogarth Press, Sigmund Freud's letter dated 19 April 1935, *Letters of Sigmund Freud, 1873–1939*; Eyre Methuen Ltd, *A Meeting by the River*, by Christopher Isherwood, copyright © 1967 by Christopher Isherwood; Elaine Greene Ltd, 'Two on a Party', published by Secker & Warburg in *Three Players of a Summer Game and Other Stories*, copyright © 1948, 1954 by Tennessee Williams; Nigel Nicolson, *Portrait of a Marriage*; The Society of Authors, as agents for the Strachey Trust, 'In Memoriam J.M.K. Ob. Sept. 1906', *Lytton Strachey*, by Michael Holroyd, Heinemann; University of Illinois Press, Kate Salt letters, *Henry Salt*, by George Hendrick; Jonathan Cape Ltd, excerpt from *Dancer from the Dance*, by Andrew Holleran.

Introduction

This book is about married homosexuals – that is, homosexual men and women who are or have been at some time in their lives legally married to a member of the opposite sex. That is the only way you can be married. Anything else, like the so-called homosexual marriage of two people of the same sex, must either be called a stable relationship or wishful thinking. There is nowhere that I have been able to discover where homosexual couples can marry in the eyes of the law and acquire the rights and duties of legal marriage.

Several years ago I wrote a book about stepparents and remarriage. Marriage, I learned from stepparents and my own experience as one, is not only a contract, but a bargain, in which many of the most important conditions are left unspoken. What do you expect to give for what you expect to get? What do you keep secret from each other? Why bother to marry at all? Do you really want children of your own?

This book presented a chance to examine many of the same questions about married life from a different perspective. Given the commitment to heterosexual intercourse that a marriage contract represents, what is the use of matrimony to someone uninterested in its basic rite?

Homosexuals may see little in common between their problems and those of stepparents, yet in fact both see themselves as departing from the traditional ideal of the nuclear family for whom the rules were written. They have a common and justifiable sense of being misunderstood: there is no admired social model to tell them how to behave. True, stepparenthood has never been against the law, but it has been the subject of one of the most virulent and persistent myths of evil in western society.

From an author's point of view, stepparents were harder

9

to find to interview, and more reluctant to talk. What if their spouse knew their real feelings for their stepchildren? Homosexuals were far more forthcoming – as individuals. As part of a political movement, however, they were suspicious of the outsider, ready to pounce at the drop of a politically incorrect word. In his book, *Homosexual Oppression and Liberation*, Dennis Altman scorns 'the heterosexual writer who ostentatiously kisses his wife and children good-bye in the first chapter before embarking on a voyeuristic tour of the homosexual world'.

It is voyeurism, I agree – but only if homosexuality is regarded as rare and freakish. I believe that what homosexuals and their spouses have to say about the marriage bond and the wish to be a parent is important to anyone interested in marriage and the family. Their dilemma raises questions that will have to be faced by a world belatedly aware, to borrow the splendid understatement of the Wolfenden Report in 1957, that homosexuals cannot reasonably be regarded as quite separate from the rest of mankind.

Much of the information for this book was drawn from forty-seven long interviews with homosexuals and with present and past wives or husbands of homosexuals. The interviews took place for the most part in New York City and Boston in the USA, and London and Manchester in England. Those who came forward, as for virtually every other kind of study about homosexuality, were volunteers, a self-selected sample. They learned about my project from letters I wrote to gay newspapers, from articles of mine in newspapers or from homophile organizations who put them in touch with me. There were dozens more than I could possibly interview, largely because of distance. Many of these wrote long, helpful letters. None of my personal acquaintances volunteered, although observing some of their marriages over the years, no questions asked, was undoubtedly another stimulus for this book.

Those who took the trouble to talk with me about their private, frequently secret, lives did so with great intensity, often with humour and sometimes with considerable sacrifice. 'I don't know why I'm doing this,' said one young man who had taken the day off work and lied to his wife in order to make the trip for the interview. But he knew, and I knew. It was the first chance he had found to talk to anyone about the conflict between his homosexuality and his marriage and his wish to be a good father. In his case and others, I have altered the details to conceal identity. But I have not changed their words. There are no phoney quotes in this book and no composite personalities. These are real people speaking.

Because homosexuality is so often equated with the outer reaches of sexual deviance – paedophilia, sado-masochism and transvestism – let me say that the homosexuals I interviewed were from the sexual middle of the road. Most were indistinguishable from heterosexuals in appearance and way of life. The men were not camp: 'The effeminate kind set my teeth on edge,' said a homosexual father of two. The women were neither butch nor, for the most part, crusading feminists. 'I hope people will just think of us as two teachers living together,' said one. A wish to be what is generally accepted as normal was, after all, one of the reasons they had married.

1

The Perfect Closet

Chainsmoking peacefully, sipping Perrier, oblivious of the flirtatious young waiter with the prep school accent, a lawyer sits in a New York restaurant searching his mind for memories of his marriage. A successful man just turned fifty, he is wearing a well-tailored three-piece grey suit. His hair is brown, his eyes blue, his cheekbones high; a face from Marlboro country. It is obvious that it is a long time since he has had to think about money or, although the two are not related, about his heterosexual past. Slowly, like someone pulling out an old blurred photograph, he retrieves his wedding day.

'It was a moment that will stay with me for all eternity. The church was full of people. My father, who was a minister, was waiting at the altar. The candles were burning. Panic swept over me. "What am I doing here?" I asked myself. My older brother, who was best man, saw the look on my face. He put his hand under my right elbow and we moved forward.'

He had not proposed to the girl who became his wife. True, they had been dating a lot. It was during the Korean war. They had both just graduated from an American midwestern university and he had just received his call-up notice. One Saturday night he and his girl came home from the movies and found their mothers sitting at the dining-room table making out lists of wedding guests.

'When the wedding day came – I think Mary was as anxious as I was – she was sick in bed with the 'flu. They were so determined to get us married that the doctor said that it was all right for her to get up to go down the aisle – but no sex for three days. My uncle who was a chemist sent us a load of contraceptives. It included a gross of rubbers, and boxes with things like "Follow instructions on label" on them. We went to our honeymoon place and

12

fell asleep exhausted. We didn't try sex for three days. When we did, it was a disaster. She was a virgin. So was I – with a woman.'

But not with a man. He had been enjoying passionate male sex since a young teacher revealed it to him at the Chicago YMCA when he was seventeen, but he had known before he was six that he was gay. When men came into the room, he sat on their laps, cuddling up to them instead of women. The first week at college, he began a homosexual relationship with someone he met in the choir. They had a long stormy affair, with infidelity and jealous arguments and tearful reconciliations. At the same time he dated girls, was a good dancer and invited Mary from his home-town up to his college for weekends. There was a lot of affection between them but no sex. As graduation day drew near, he broke up with his lover and moved away from all his gay friends except one who was getting married.

'At the friend's wedding, I was best man. Mary was in the wedding party. Before it we had a lot of discussion, this friend and I, about marriage. We felt that, once we were married, that would be that. We'd move away from homosexuality. We all, all the gay friends I had at college, felt that.'

So, apparently, did his family, although his homosexuality was not mentioned in that strict religious environment and that puritanical time. However, one day his brother took him for a long drive in the country, finally stopping the car and declaring, 'I'm going to take this demon out of you!'

'I said, knowing what he meant, "Don't. You can't. It's not a demon. It's me." He was bitterly angry but I thought to myself, "At least I've got a brother" – because he had always been very remote. What he did was go to my father and say, "If we get him married, everything will be all right."' The wedding followed soon after.

Homosexual? Married? In spite of the obvious evidence in history and everyday life, the two states are still thought to be a contradiction in terms. When initiating a lawsuit for libel in 1980 against a man who had called him gay on a

13

television talk show, Cary Grant exclaimed, 'How can they say I'm gay? I've been married four times!' On a BBC radio programme, someone gets a laugh from mentioning Ronald Reagan's son who 'surprised everybody by getting married when they had all thought he was a confirmed ballet dancer'. To counteract the publicity from a lawsuit claiming that the tennis star Billie Jean King had lived in a lesbian relationship for more than seven years, an official of the Women's Tennis Association declared that Mrs King's marriage was 'sound'.

To people who believe that homosexuality is an evil that should be suppressed, it may seem improbable that anyone tries to hide homosexuality in a day and age when homosexuals parade their cause, flaunt their predilection in television comedies and advertise for partners in newspapers. Yet most homosexuals are not militant, nor even active in pursuing gay rights. Even if they are frank and openly acknowledged as homosexuals as the lawyer just mentioned, they still live in a world where prejudice remains strong and the penalties against homosexual behaviour in many places are harsh. A great many of American states still classify homosexual acts as sodomy, punishable, in theory at least, by prison terms of many years. In Britain, where homosexual acts in private between consenting adults have been legal since 1967, liberalization has been hedged with enough qualifications to give police ample excuse for harassing homosexuals. 'Adults', for homosexuals in Britain, means people over the age of twenty-one, while the legal age of consent for heterosexuals is only sixteen; 'in private' means that no third party may be present, even in an adjoining room. And if the homosexual behaviour takes place in the military service or merchant marine, or in Northern Ireland, it is still as criminal under the law as it was before the reform.

These persisting sanctions reinforce the homosexual's most powerful motive for concealment: to avoid being considered 'queer' and being excluded from ordinary society. The fact is, therefore, that for anyone wishing to hide homosexuality, marriage is the best closet. A wedding

14

ring is still a requirement for many jobs to do with children.
Bachelorhood remains suspect. 'Not the marrying kind'
these days means 'not that way inclined'. In 1972 the US
National Institute of Mental Health report backed folk
wisdom with statistics: half or more of college-educated
males still unmarried by the age of forty, it calculated, have
had overt homosexual contact.

If marriage is the badge of heterosexuality, then parenthood is the gold medal. Its value is even accepted by
spouses who might otherwise have their doubts. A housewife and mother recalled at a self-help group for wives of
homosexuals how she and her husband were sitting in front
of the television one evening and saw on the news the
picture of a member of the royal family.

' "They say he's homosexual," said my husband.

' "But he's got children," I said.

' "That doesn't prove anything," said my husband.

'Then I thought about his friend Hal, who'd been
hanging around the house for three years. I took a deep
breath and asked, "What about you, then?" '

'Back came his answer: "I don't want to hurt you." '

In the popular mind, homosexuality has been associated
with marriage only as its mortal enemy. It has been seen as
a threat to the home and the family since antiquity. While
the Greeks may have admired the homosexual love of an
older man for a beautiful, beardless youth, they placed
highest value on marriage and family life; heterosexuality
was the norm and homosexuality was not seen as an
alternative way of life for two adult men or women. None of
Homer's heroes has homosexual lovers.

Just how specifically the Old Testament condemned
homosexuality is still the subject of lively debate among
biblical scholars. Did the condemnation in Leviticus –
'Thou shalt not lie with mankind, as with womankind: it is
an abomination' (18:22) – mean that it was evil or merely
unclean? Was the sin of the Sodomites homosexuality,
rape – or inhospitality? But the moral teachings of traditional Judaism and Catholicism leave no room for doubt. St
Thomas Aquinas laid down the law to clear away all

confusion: all acts not leading to procreation are unnatural and evil. Since then the supposed enmity between homosexual and family life has been stated again and again, the more vehemently by the more puritanical societies. The Nazis, the Russians, the Chinese and the Irish have all attacked homosexuality for undermining the home and family. It is not clear what the dominant fear is – loss of population or seduction of the young.

In 1980, in an article in the American Jewish intellectual monthly, *Commentary*, that infuriated many readers, the writer Midge Decter portrayed a camp and increasingly aggressive homosexual society which sneers at the straight world, and drives families into retreat. Middle-class surburban audiences, she observed, have applauded homosexual plays (such as *Who's Afraid of Virginia Woolf?*) for being profound statements about modern family life. 'Women have permitted themselves to be rendered breastless, and men to become pocketbook carriers, by homosexual designers.' Fathers, she said, feel devalued by gay men. They see themselves as paunchy and mortgage-ridden in contrast to the slimness and affluence of the men without families.

Thus heterosexuality and homosexuality looked poles apart even from her perspective of Manhattan, 1980. Why this should be so is a mystery. The two kinds of life have always been entwined. While the bronzed bachelor sunning himself in bikini trunks is the one who gets noticed, there are many other hidden, married homosexuals, quietly carrying out all their domestic responsibilities. Marriage should never have been taken as proof of being straight. The Yale historian, John Boswell, in *Christianity, Social Tolerance and Homosexuality*, quotes the frankness with which monkist chronicles recorded the sexual orientation of the idol of chivalry, Richard Lion Heart:

Richard, [then] duke of Aquitaine, son of the king of England, remained with Philip, the king of France, who so honored him for so long that they ate every day at the same table and from the same dish, and at night their beds did not separate them. And the king of France loved him as his own soul; and they loved each other so much that the king of England was

16

absolutely astonished at the passionate love between them and marveled at it.

Richard did penance several times for 'that sin' (*'peccatum illud'*), and did marry, but the fact that he left no children was widely interpreted as a sign of lack of consummation.

Boswell argues that only those societies which insist that erotic energy be focused on one's permanent legal spouse would expect gay people to forgo marriage and children. In more tolerant societies such as the Roman or the medieval, he maintains, gay people married and begat just like everybody else. Boswell's scholarship would be even more impressive if it did not appear to be marshalled for an attack on anti-gay prejudice in modern society. He may have overstated his case, however, for a truly tolerant society may in reality be the one which allows gay people the freedom *not* to marry, exempting them from the traditional social obligations to produce heirs and pass on property. For example, the historian Laurence Stone has remarked on a distinct change in the marriage patterns of the English aristocracy between the late sixteenth and late seventeenth centuries. In the earlier period the eldest son and heir married almost without exception; the obligations of primogeniture required it, just as it compelled many younger sons with no property to remain bachelors. Yet the public records show an abrupt rise in bachelor squires, starting about a century later. Some of these men, Stone speculates, may have been homosexual, and in the free and easy atmosphere of the Restoration, they may have been more open in acknowledging their preferences and in resisting marriage.

The roster of married homosexuals is star-studded – many Roman emperors (Julius Caesar was known as 'husband to every man's wife and wife to every woman's husband'); certain English kings, most flagrant of whom were Edward II, father of four, and James I ('James the Queen'), father of seven; Tchaikovsky, Frederick the Great, John Maynard Keynes (about whom more later) and Hart Crane; many great names from the entertainment world of whom only the dead can be mentioned in print, such as

Tyrone Power; and even – if the passion of her letters to her long-time companion, Lorena Hickok, were translated into action – Eleanor Roosevelt.

Today married homosexuals constitute the dark furtive side of homosexuality. Most do not brave the gay bars or clubs which can be found not only in London's Soho and Earls Court but in what might seem the unlikely places of Truro, Belfast and Stoke-on-Trent. If they are men, they lead their homosexual lives as often as not in public lavatories, balconies of cinemas, parks and tow paths. If they are women, they simply do not tell their husbands. That so many homosexuals remain silent and hidden may seem implausible but they are there in their thousands, caught between the gay world and the straight, sometimes contented, sometimes living double lives, risking blackmail and exposure and the break-up of their families.

How many . . .? What proportion of . . .? People who rush in with these obvious questions have been reading about other phenomena in Social Trends, like unmarried mothers or the ownership of television sets. The least appreciated fact about homosexuality is that nobody's counting. It is still taboo to count. There has been no systematic attempt to calculate the incidence of homosexuality in the general population in Britain and none in the United States since Kinsey published *Sexual Behaviour in the Human Male* in 1948.

It is a measure of Kinsey's achievement that his statistics are more widely accepted and used today than they were in the early postwar days of romantic movies and virginity, when his research was ridiculed and read as a dirty book. Kinsey, who was a sober monogamous entomologist, wondered at the characteristic of the human mind 'to dichotomize in its classification of phenomena', particularly into homosexual versus heterosexual. 'Many persons do not want to believe that there are gradations in these matters from one to the other extreme.' To break down the arbitrary split and to substitute a more useful way of measuring the degree of an individual's sexual preference, he designed his scale. The Kinsey scale ranges from 0 to 6. People with no homosexual experience are classified as Kinsey 0. Those with nothing but are Kinsey 6. Those with mixed experience are distributed somewhere in between.

A far greater number of men than the macho-America of 1948 was willing to accept had had, according to Kinsey, homosexual contact to the point of orgasm between adolescence and old age – more than one-third (37 per cent) of the total white male population, he ventured. Ten per cent of white males were more or less exclusively homosexual for three years between sixteen and fifty-five and about 4 per cent of white males remained exclusively homosexual throughout their lives.

Kinsey recognized that there were a lot of married homosexuals. Among the married men his team interviewed, the incidence of homosexuality was nearly 11 per cent of those between the ages of twenty-one and twenty-five; this proportion dropped to 2 per cent among those around the age of forty-five. Conscious of the difficulty of getting honest answers about forbidden activity, Kinsey acknowledged that the true incidence of homosexuality among the married was probably much higher. 'Married males,' he observed, 'who have social position to maintain and who fear that their wives may discover their extra-marital activities are not readily persuaded into contributing histories to research studies.' What he could be sure of was that he and his associates had listened to hundreds of younger men telling of their homosexual contacts with older, socially established, married males.

Lesbians, under the Kinsey calculations in *Sexual Behaviour in the Human Female* in 1953, were seen as less prone to marry than were male homosexuals, just as lesbian experience was estimated to have involved a smaller proportion of the female population as a whole – 13 per cent. However, today these findings distress the lesbian activists, who exclaim, 'How can anybody say there are three times as many male homosexuals as female? It just stands to reason that the proportions must be equal!'

The more recent major study by the Kinsey Institute for

Sex Research in the San Francisco Bay Area, whose results were published in 1978 as *Homosexualities* by Alan Bell and Martin Weinberg, and are also widely quoted abroad, suggested that whatever the general incidence, the female variety of homosexuality is hidden more frequently in the closet of marriage.

Of the nearly 1,000 homosexuals interviewed, the San Francisco Kinsey Institute Study found that, while one-fifth of the men had been married at some time in their lives, the comparable figures for women were one-third of the white lesbians and nearly half of the black. One explanation for the difference between the behaviour of homosexuals of the two sexes (a difference which will be referred to in many of the following pages) is that the women tended not to realize they were homosexual until after they married. Most of the men, in contrast, knew or had suspected they were gay in adolescence, if not even earlier.

Any gay switchboard (a publicly advertised telephone counselling and reference centre) is used to receiving telephone box calls from panicky married people, asking in the same breath; 'What should I do?' and 'Should I tell my husband?' (or wife). The generally accepted answer among gay advisers is diametrically opposite for the two sexes. For men, it tends to be 'Consider telling your wife. She probably knows already.' For women it is, 'Don't tell your husband until you have custody of the children.'

In many ways homosexuality caricatures and exaggerates the difference between the sexes. Homosexual men are overwhelmingly more promiscuous than homosexual women. The 1978 figures from San Francisco (which will be referred to as the Kinsey Institute Study, to distinguish it from the 1948 and 1953 Kinsey reports, prepared by a team that included Kinsey himself) revealed that many homosexual men often paid for sex, did not know the partner's name and picked up people under sixteen. Nearly two-thirds had had venereal disease or hepatitis. In contrast, the women were homebodies. Most had fewer than a dozen women lovers. Few looked for partners – what homosexuals call 'cruising' – in public places. None had caught VD.

For married men with homosexual tastes, what these habits mean is a heavy reliance on anonymous sex in public places. The extent of the practice has been well documented by the American sociologist and clergyman, Laud Humphreys, in a book called *Tearoom Trade*. 'Tearooms' are, in American gay slang, what 'cottages' are in British – public lavatories frequented by homosexuals. Humphreys systematically observed a number of men engaged in performing or receiving oral sex in public lavatories in one nameless American city. Then, by writing down the licence plate numbers of the men's cars as they drove away, and by enlisting police cooperation on the pretext of conducting an uncontroversial survey about health, Humphreys was able to trace his subjects' home addresses and to interview them there to find out what manner of men they were.

The majority were married men living with their wives. The marriages did not seem to be shaky. There was no sign that the wives suspected their husbands' double lives. From all the outward appearances, these were just the people next door. How widespread is this clandestine activity? In his book, Humphreys ventured his own answer based on the city where he did his observations: 5 per cent of the total male population. (Most of these men, he found, as have similar investigations, did not in any way consider themselves homosexual.)

If this estimate is anywhere near the truth, if at the very least 4 per cent of the population is homosexual and if more lesbians than male homosexuals find their way into the married state, the total numbers of married homosexuals in Britain must be at least in the hundreds of thousands. In other words, the homosexual husband or wife must be neither an absurdity nor an anachronism but an invisible common variation among the patterns of marriage.

2

What's in a Label?

In Kingsley Amis's *Lucky Jim*, as Jim is about to steal Christine away from the creep Bertrand, he asks her, 'Are you in love with him?'

> 'I don't much care for that word,' she said, as if rebuking a foul-mouthed tradesman.
> 'Why not?'
> 'Because I don't know what it means.'
> He gave a quiet yell. 'Oh don't say that; no don't say that. It's a word you must often have come across in conversation and literature. Are you going to tell me it sends you flying to the dictionary each time?'

Nobody should have to fly to the dictionary to look up 'homosexual'. It means having a sexual preference for your own sex and that is how it will be used in this book. Sociologists writing about homosexuality, however, labour in order to account for the difference between action and fantasy (many people are in fact homosexual as others are adulterers – only in their hearts) and also to encompass the fact that so many men and women have had both kinds of experience. In search of precision, what sociologists invent are not words but rather verbal formulas, such as this gem taken from Judd Marmor's *Homosexual Behaviour*: 'one who is motivated in adult life by a definite preferential erotic attraction to members of the same sex and who usually (but not necessarily) engages in overt sexual relations with them'.

In everyday speech, however, even social scientists use the word 'homosexual' without difficulty – as an adjective. Where the rot of ambiguity sets in is using it as a noun. To be 'a homosexual' is to be in a fixed category and nowhere else. The noun 'homosexual' also implies action rather than fantasy. Believers in a traditional religion know very well

22

the difference that lies between the two uses of the word – it is no less than that between sin and grace. The religions which classify homosexual acts as evil, yet which would be lost without the hundreds of thousands of gay men who carry on their work, believe that there is nothing sinful in being 'homosexual' in inclination, but that it is totally forbidden to be 'a homosexual' in practice.

Thus the fight goes on in many quarters to be labelled a person with homosexual tendencies rather than a homosexual *per se*. When, in 1979, the former leader of the Liberal Party, Jeremy Thorpe, successfully defended himself against the charge of conspiracy to murder Norman Scott, a male model who had accused him of seducing him into a lengthy affair, the defence lawyer conceded that Thorpe, a twice-married man, had had 'homosexual tendencies' – a failing known to the ancient Greeks – which had ruined Thorpe's political career. The same formulation was used in 1980 by Congressman Robert Bauman of Maryland, a Republican conservative. Arrested for soliciting from a teenage boy, Bauman appeared with his wife and priest to confess to the press 'homosexual tendencies' which he blamed on drink.

If 'homosexual' can prove confusing, what about 'bisexual'? '"Bi-guy" seeks roommate', reads a newspaper ad. What is he and what does he want? There is no guidance in common speech, and still less from the experts. One psychiatrist defines bisexuals as people who are sexually attracted to and have sexual relationships with both men and women. Other people use the term for anyone who has had even one encounter outside his or her usual preference. A mass of free-floating clichés clouds the issue: 'Freud said we are all bisexual' and 'Doesn't everybody go through a homosexual phase?' Yet whatever these phrases might mean, it is obvious that everybody is not bisexual, in the sense of seeking sexual contact to the point of orgasm with either sex impartially.

The search for a clear meaning of 'bisexual' is complicated by the fact that many people, in situations of sexual deprivation, such as prison or the army, will resort to what psychologists call 'situational homosexuality', which dis-

23

appears when the deprivation ends. Are they bisexual or just adaptive? In despair, the sex researchers Masters and Johnson decided that bisexuality was of no use as a label: it means, they found, whatever an individual wants it to mean. However, in their major study of homosexual response, they did discover a dozen people who could be described as genuine neutrals, who liked one sex just as well as the other. As a group, these had unique characteristics: they were not only impartial but loners, uncommitted to any one person. Most of them had never married. Masters and Johnson decided to give them a label of their own: ambisexuals. These were (Masters and Johnson's prose beggars parody) 'a man or a woman who unreservedly enjoys, solicits, or responds to overt sexual opportunity with equal ease and interest regardless of the sex of the partners, and who, as a sexually mature individual, has never evidenced interest in a continuing relationship'.

What might seem just a superficial matter of labels actually raises fundamental questions of basic identity. People want to know what they are. During many of the interviews for this book, it became apparent that for many people 'bisexual' is a more comfortable label because it does not carry the exclusion from heterosexual society that 'homosexual' does. Beyond a doubt, the wives of homosexuals prefer 'bisexual'. For example, a London salesman who describes himself as 'a happily married homosexual' and who has been homosexually active for eight years, recounted an exchange with his wife: 'I knew I was gay for a long time. I discussed it with my wife. "I wonder if I'm homosexual," I said. "Nonsense," she said. "You're bisexual. You make love to me, don't you?"'

In contrast, many married men and women who find themselves overwhelmed by a passion for their own sex are joyful about their discovery. They have that born-again feeling; they want to tell the world. They call themselves homosexual even though they continue to perform their marital obligations: 'I enjoy sex with my wife. I've taught myself to enjoy it. But for that boom-boom, it's men.' And: 'I realize I've been a lesbian all my life. My husband

24

doesn't know I'm gay. Just because I'm a lesbian doesn't mean I can't have sex with men. That's just not the way I want to be.'

On the American top-ranking television programme, *Sixty Minutes*, Mike Wallace interviewed an Englishman who had taken a male lover while still living with his wife: 'And you, Gerry – are you bisexual or are you basically homosexual?' Gerry replied, 'I think I'm basically homosexual. I mean let me put it like this, I think if our relationship ended for some reason, I would find it impossible to form a sexual relationship with another female.'

Then, too, committed homosexuals or bisexuals resent people adopting their labels, if they are really heterosexuals in disguise. Said one lesbian contemptuously about an acquaintance: 'I don't call a woman who fucks three men bisexual!'

Many people swiftly conclude that homosexuals who marry must stand somewhere between 3 and 5 on Kinsey's scale and should all be labelled bisexual. They are wrong. Even Kinsey 6s do occasionally marry. A London clergyman, for example, who has lived in a *ménage à trois* with his lover and his lover's wife for many years, insists that were his lover to die, he would ask the widow to marry him. She is a woman whom he would be happy to have as a wife. 'But I'm not one bit heterosexual,' he says engagingly. 'A heterosexual thought has never crossed my mind.'

The simplest way out of the terminological thicket seems to be to let people define themselves. If they say they are bisexual or lesbian they must mean it. In general, for the purposes of this book, 'homosexual' will be used to refer to preference, without implying exclusive homosexual activity. And homosexuals will often be referred to by the word they have chosen for themselves – gay.

'Gay' may be the most controversial word of all. Even some with homosexual experience reject it. 'To be gay,' said one man, 'means being too thin, wearing funny underwear and going to Mykonos.' In other words, camp (extravagant and bizarre) and effeminate. Many psychiatrists refuse the word, maintaining that gay stands for the very opposite of what homosexuals feel and is a cover for homosexual depression. For their part, many heterosexuals are furious at the loss of a good strong word from the general vocabulary. 'Do we have to use the happy word "gay" to describe the dissolute or the disorientated?' asked a vicar in a letter to the *Daily Telegraph*. Yet homosexuals have needed a word that is neither coldly scientific nor pejoratively slangy like fairy, pansy and fag. If they represent – at the most cautious estimate – one out of twenty-five people in the population; and if in the past decade the biggest gain for homosexuals has been in self-respect, then they seem to deserve a plain, ordinary word with which to describe themselves. Their takeover of the word 'gay' has helped that progress and the language's loss has been social justice's gain. In the pages that follow, people are described as what they say they are, and many of them say they are gay.

3

Just Best Friends

With the single-mindedness that some women bring to finding their daughters a husband, Lucy and Margaret labour to keep their husbands lovers. Their two marriages are twinned like binary stars, for the sake of the children and for, both wives say, their own happiness. Their husbands are their best friends; they cannot imagine life without them.

When Lucy met George in 1968 at a Church of England youth club, she was twenty-nine, the manager of an office for a small oil company, and he was twenty-two, a social worker at the church. They were friendly enough for about two years but Lucy ruled George out as a prospective date because of the difference in their ages and besides, while she was lonely and had always longed to find somebody to share her life with, she liked her independence and the new flat she was still doing up and she was not actively looking for a husband. Then, with Christmas approaching, both were put on a small committee to arrange a party with food, for fifty or sixty people. Lucy noticed that George telephoned her more often than the catering justified. Things began to sparkle between them at the party. Lucy remembers being absolutely shattered at what she felt happening: 'Oh, God,' she thought, 'how can I feel a sexual attraction to somebody so young, this little boy, and me, the mature career woman?'

While the attraction was undeniably sexual and they began sleeping together, what impressed both of them was their boundless and unexpected compatibility of interests. George said he had never found anybody like Lucy. She felt the same: 'It was like a meeting of souls.' It was only when George revealed that he had been planning to take a year's trip to the Far East that the gap in their ages intruded. At twenty-four, he wanted to see the world, yet, astonishing to both of them, he found he could not bear to go without her.

27

He asked Lucy to come with him. Neither of them thought of getting married. Its legal implications put them off. Lucy did not want to travel – it was like turning the clock back – but after a traumatic few months, she decided to give up her job, let her flat, and off they went.

They wandered the world, hitchhiked, slept in tents, made friends, and even managed to save a little money. Their sex life was active, if not passionate. Lucy, who had had one affair before, knew that it was by no means perfect but thought it was lovely because it was George.

To this day neither of them can quite explain why, when they returned home, they got married. It wasn't family pressure because their families were quite tolerant about their trip. It certainly wasn't pressure from friends. Well, perhaps there was some subtle suggestion from Lucy's parents with whom they stayed for a while after their return, and who had put George on a camp bed downstairs while Lucy slept in a room upstairs. That seemed ridiculous. After a year's travelling together, they felt they had seen the best and worst of each other and had each found the person they wanted to live with for the rest of their lives. In her own mind Lucy felt very fortunate and wondered what she had done to deserve George because she knew she was not an easy person to get along with. Still, they cherished the idea of themselves as unorthodox. Was it she who said the words, 'Let's get married'? Maybe what she said was less specific, something like 'Let's conform.' The last thing they wanted was to waste money on a wedding. When the time came to go to the civil ceremony, they went on bicycles.

For the first months of their marriage, they lived in Lucy's flat. It had only one room. Next thing they knew they found themselves in a house in suburbia. The house was a good buy, a neat redbrick in a cul de sac, double-lined with identical houses with hydrangeas and television aerials, and near a station where George could catch the train every day to town. Lucy in particular was overwhelmed by the feeling of inappropriateness. 'We had set ourselves up as a typical suburban couple which I never felt we were.'

The typical suburban couple has children. Once again Lucy and George fought the stereotype. Frankly, they did not know whether they wanted children or not. They were having a lovely time. Lucy still likes to think back on it. 'George and I had loads of social life, many good friends whom we would visit. We loved walking in the country and we liked visiting old churches and historical houses. We used to go out most week-ends. We both love the outdoors.' After about a year, Lucy found uneasiness creeping over her. She was then thirty-four. Would she regret it later if she didn't have a child? Perhaps if she hadn't pushed George . . . he certainly was not as eager as she soon became . . . but he agreed to throw caution to the winds and she came off the Pill. Nothing happened. Their consciences were relieved, they didn't have to make any decisions. Lucy was offered a new job teaching bookkeeping in the evening, which would give them even more money.

Then Lucy's period was late. So much time had gone by since she had used contraception that she didn't honestly believe it was pregnancy. She went for a test. When they told her it was positive, the news was almost like a physical blow. They had said the words so matter-of-factly and her whole life was changed for ever more. In a daze she walked home to tell George. Shock turned to panic, then to resignation. Eight months later their son Jimmy was born.

Totally immersed in the experience of childbirth, Lucy did not foresee what was coming: 'During my pregnancy, George went off sex completely. Our sexual relations weren't all that brilliant anyhow. Not once a week, no, more like once a month. It hadn't bothered me very much, just sometimes. I don't have a very high libido. Maybe I would if I were married to somebody who really turned me on. When I had my affair, my libido then was very brisk, very, very good. But I think the less and less sex you have, you just wind yourself down.

'Anyway, we had no sex at all while I was carrying Jimmy which I began to find annoying because I became quite sexy when I was pregnant. Afterwards, our sex life resumed its normal quality, but I always felt it was me that

29

was probably initiating it. Whenever I felt turned on, I would sort of try and get the old vibrations going across the bed and turn George on. By then he was terribly inhibited sexually, but this didn't bother me. It's no use somebody pretending something they don't feel. In his teens he had had problems with his sexuality, he had told me that he had gone through "a phase" as he put it, and wondered if he were homosexual. But still, I thought that's a normal stage that most people go through. Probably he's got a few hang-ups.

'So there we were, with a not very active sex life and Jimmy two and a half, when I had a miscarriage. That upset George a lot more than I knew at the time. For quite a long time afterwards I did become depressed, but I suddenly had this compelling urge to get pregnant again. It was horrible. I didn't want George for himself at all. I just wanted another baby inside me. I can understand the urge that propels the rapist now. I was watching the foolish calendar, something I'd never done before. I was more or less forcing George to make love to me at the appropriate time, and getting all uptight when he didn't want to. He'd just be going off to sleep and I'd say, "You silly fool, it's tonight! It's got to be tonight, George!"

'It was terrible but it worked. Claire was conceived on the Saturday morning when I thought, "This has got to be it, I've got to do it this month." Then, of course, I didn't bother at all any more because once he knew I was pregnant, George was definitely not interested in sex at all. One way and another George had a pretty awful year. He caught some bug that affected his whole system; he got into such a state that I had to actually physically take him to the doctor. Then his brother was killed in a car crash. Towards the end of my pregnancy George became more and more remote. I thought it was because he was grieving about his brother. That was strange, because he was never terribly close to his brother, but such feelings were very foreign to me as I am an only child.

'The baby was born in September. Just before Christmas George was a real write-off. I knew something was wrong. Always on Thursday nights, he used to go to an evening

30

class and on Sunday mornings for a walk. Always. I know George is a private person and I know he does need solitude. Home was noisy. It did used to hurt me that he could still go out when I needed him to help me cope with the baby and Jimmy. I just thought, "How can you be so selfish?" It was entirely out of character and he always came back for Sunday lunch.

'As Jimmy grew old enough to trot along, sometimes George would take him on his Sunday walk. One day, he said, "While we were out, we met this fellow who was walking a dog. Jimmy became quite friendly with the dog and so we went for a walk together." After that, sometimes I'd say, "Did you meet the man with the dog?" and he'd say, "Oh yes, he was there." The man's name was Dave.

'Then George would sometimes bring Jimmy back early and ask, "Can you take care of him? Dave and I are going for a drink," and I thought, "Great. That sounds nice," because George didn't really have any men friends that I knew about. I thought, "Oh, at long last, you've found a man you can talk to."Dave was married with four kids, so obviously, as we women do sometimes, you offload your problems onto one another and it seemed quite above board and honest. Then some Sundays George would say, "It's a bad day today. I won't take Jimmy, Dave's got a few problems he wants to talk over with me," and this is how it went on. He didn't take Jimmy any more. He made an extra effort to dress up and always went on the dot of ten for his damned walk. I don't know where I thought they were walking but there was something at the back of my mind that something was wrong.

'He was getting more and more uptight. One night, about six weeks before Christmas, I'd got to bed early and he came in late. I could sense that he was in a bad way. He didn't say, "Are you awake?" or anything like that. He just crawled into bed beside me and started crying. And went on crying, desperately. I put my arms around him and tried to comfort him. "What am I going to do?" he cried. Suddenly I knew. "It's got something to do with Dave, hasn't it?" "That was very perceptive of you," he said and broke down

31

again. Then out it poured. "I'm homosexual. I'm in love with Dave and I don't know what to do." His actual words were, "I'm a homosexual", not "I'm gay". "It is just something that I've known for some time now, but I didn't deliberately intend for this to happen."

'"This" was falling in love. His homosexuality he had kept away from me but this he couldn't – he cared equally for someone else as for me.

'It was just as though it was all happening to someone else, or I was watching it on television. It was so unreal. I wasn't angry or shocked; the only emotion I had was compassion. I just felt so terribly sorry for him and my whole inside was churned up. I felt so desperately sorry and I thought to myself, "Lucy, what *can* we do? What *can* we do! There he is, just an absolute schizophrenic, in love with two people, desperately in love with this . . . this other man." From the pillow beside me George kept repeating, "I don't want to give him up. I just can't give him up."'

Still as if from a distance, Lucy's mind kept lecturing her. 'You can't be that cruel as to tell him to give him up, Lucy, you can't pretend the situation doesn't exist. It is there. So which is the best way to cope with it?'

When they woke up in the morning, Lucy wondered if it all had been a dream. They both got up and without talking much or looking directly at each other went through their breakfast ritual and George left for work. Lucy recalls:

'I didn't know what to do. I had my two children to look after. I didn't phone anybody. I was in a state of shock. Every time I thought of the children, I just kept breaking down, that's what really got to me. Every time I looked at Jimmy I would start to howl. I just desperately wanted my children to have a stable upbringing and happy family life with stable relationships. I didn't think of walking out and taking the children. No, no. It didn't alter my feelings for George. I still loved him. He was still George. He had this nightmarish problem, loving two people. If there was any thought that burned, it was that he could love someone else than me. The fact that it was another man was irrelevant. As much as I'd wanted a better sex life, the thought of

32

another man had never crossed my mind because we had made a vow. Not in a church, but what did that matter? I went into a marriage intending to keep myself only for him for the rest of my life, and I thought he did too.'

That day Lucy's cousin, the closest she ever came to having a sister, did drop over. She had just gone through a divorce, and as she unburdened herself, Lucy thought guiltily that no longer would they share intimate secrets with one another. 'Where's George?' asked the cousin and Lucy had to say, 'His class.' The lying had begun.

'I felt I had to lie to her because I didn't think my cousin was equipped to understand homosexuality. In the course of any conversation, I began to be aware, gayness can crop up. Everybody has the idea of a gay person as effeminate and uncommon and perverted. As we talked, I thought how I would have to pretend, which was entirely foreign to me. I'd always worn my heart on my sleeve. Now I can't.

'What I really wanted to do was to phone Dave's wife, whose name was Margaret. I didn't know how to contact her, but I desperately wanted to talk. "My God," I thought, "she has four children! To cope with this!" When I talked to George about my wish, he said that Dave was coming over on Sunday and that he would like to bring Margaret to meet me. I said "Oh yes please." Suddenly it was Sunday and all three – Dave, George and Margaret – walked in the door.'

When George married Lucy, he was not a double dealer. 'I wasn't trying to fool anybody,' he says, 'I just suppose I successfully fooled myself . . . for a while. I had had contact with other men, but I had written these off as unimportant – as a lot of homosexuals seem to do: they think, "It's a temporary thing, but not really me." It never really crossed my mind, growing up, that homosexuality would disqualify me for marriage. When the thoughts got too uncomfortable I just shut them out. I don't remember the exact date that homosexuality first entered my mind; but I must have been quite young. Like all boys, I was conditioned to think that I would like women. I cut a photograph of a semi-naked woman out of the newspapers and I had it by the side of my bed. All boys of that age tend to masturbate quite a lot – I tried to make myself interested in this way. But it didn't take. There was always a man in the background.

'When I did find myself responding to men, I thought it was temporary. I was taught all these classical Freudian things (which nobody has disproved) where people go through stages of development that include a homosexual one. When I was very young, we had a neighbour with two boys, one of them the same age as me. On Saturday evenings their parents used to go out for a drink and as they had a television and I didn't, I used to go there to watch television, and there was definitely some sort of sexual interest, displaying our equipment and whatever boys of that age are interested in. This boy I haven't seen for many years, but I am sure he has grown up heterosexual. At least, I know he's married and got two children . . . Anyway, at about the age of fifteen, one night when I came in, the older boy was dressed up and looking very smart and I felt physically attracted to him, which hadn't really happened before.

'I only had three or four girlfriends. The serious one who had preceded Lucy, when I was about eighteen, worked with me. She was about three years older – I seem to go for girls who are older – and I think she had had quite a lot of experience. She wanted to get married. It frightened me because I found her sort of demanding with her emotions. My feeling was not one of recoil. I've never been repulsed by women at all, I've always found them very pleasant to be with, and still do. I'm not really sexually attracted to them, but I am attracted to their femininity, good looks and charm.

'When I met Lucy, I used to go to her place quite a lot for meals in the evenings and then stay until about four in the morning. It wasn't accepted in the late 1960s to spend the night. I'm sure my mother would have been happier if I had. She said, "I don't care what you do but do try and get more sleep." Because I looked so terrible in the morning.'

George laughs confidently and happily; it is a good

memory. 'Well, my sexual relationship with Lucy during that time was very active and enjoyable. I thought that this was the best I'd ever find and I was quite happy. I didn't believe all the passion bit; I didn't believe half the things I'd read were true. I thought they were people's fantasies.'

With great effort, George can bring himself to acknowledge that he was having homosexual encounters during this time. As he reconstructs it, 'Ye–es. it was happening. I don't think it was happening at the beginning. I mean, it had happened before I met Lucy. Not very often because I was too nervous. With strangers. Some of them I saw a second time. Yes, oh, yes. This sounds terribly sordid. While we were travelling, we were walking with some friends and I said, "Excuse me, I must find a toilet." There was one along the street and I went down into it. It was summertime and very hot and there was somebody obviously displaying his wares. It rather threw me, and the feeling was very unwelcome, because I was very attracted. I knew it happened all over the world, particularly in Arab countries. I did get my bottom pinched in Morocco by a man – well, there weren't any women around, and I thought, "Well, that's never happened before."

'I have a mental block about these months until we moved to the suburbs. I became aware that near the station I use there is a public toilet which is obviously a meeting place for homosexuals. It's just terrible that that has to be. I wasn't aware then that there were any gay clubs, and I don't think I would have had the confidence. So that was the only type of meeting place possible. It's a form of self-protection. You've got a valid excuse for going to the toilet. Anyway, I did meet two or three people that I saw fairly regularly but it was . . . purely sexual. I couldn't just sort of go with anybody. They had to be people I liked and attractive to me. Before Dave, there was somebody I saw for about a year, but I never really got any satisfactory emotional relationship going. None of these relationships seemed a threat to what I had with Lucy because they were mere sexual relief. Then I met Dave.

'As far as looks go, I thought that Dave was out of this

world. I couldn't believe that anyone as attractive as that would be interested in me. I still find it hard to believe that I'm physically attractive. People keep saying I am, but it doesn't help when you don't believe it yourself. I took Dave back to the flat that an older gay friend, unmarried, had loaned me. Dave was very tense and emotional and I sensed he had these deep feelings. I think it grew on that, really. I knew he was married, that he was under great strain and that his wife knew about him. He didn't have any friends because he always stopped short in case anyone found out he was homosexual. To start with, I felt very sorry for him.

'This sounds very big-headed, I know, but I think I may be the only one so far to have given Dave self-confidence. It wasn't an easy relationship to start with. There were great traumas. Neither of us believed it was all happening. It was far stronger than anything that had ever hit me. I just couldn't hide it from Lucy. The thought of hiding it just became awful. Here was somebody that I felt just as strong for in my emotions as I did for her. I suppose that was the true acceptance of myself being homosexual. I just didn't believe that what I had with Dave existed. I thought I had reached the ultimate with Lucy.

'Today the sexual side is still very strong but we also just enjoy going out together, being close to each other, walking down the road. What do we talk about? If you're not careful, it just ends up talking about the situation we're in.

'When my brother died, I was devastated because he was the same age as Dave. "God," I thought, "is something going to happen to Dave before we ever get a chance to have our life together?"'

When Margaret walked into Lucy's living-room, Lucy's first thought was that they were not natural allies. To Lucy, Margaret, shy, pretty and neat with glasses, was very typical, the model of the suburban housewife – mother. They didn't have much in common at all, she thought, except their one colossal problem.

The atmosphere was very strained. Margaret held everything back and sat upright, very tense. She didn't seem able to communicate with Dave in the easy way that George and Lucy had with each other. Dave didn't make a good impression at all and Lucy was astonished to find that to her he looked quite obviously homosexual. They just started to talk, keeping the conversation floating around their children and the house and the weather. They all desperately wanted to talk about homosexuality but none would take the plunge. It was left to George to suggest that Dave come upstairs to see Jimmy's train set and the two wives were left together.

'Well, how long have you known?' Lucy asked.

'About eleven years,' Margaret said.

Margaret met Dave at a dance when he was in the Air Force. He was good-looking, and she was delighted when he asked her to dance. She was not a virgin; she had had a boy friend before Dave, and nearly got engaged, had sex and enjoyed it. Sleeping with Dave was even better. They didn't use any contraception but got away with it until, as happens to many couples, they got married. Then the babies kept turning up – the first, nine months later, the second the following year, and after a gap two more.

If Dave was ever restless or disappointed, he didn't show it. He went to work in his father's dry cleaner's, even though he didn't like the old man – a small-town tycoon – who snorted when Dave said he thought he might like to go to art school. Their families lived near each other. Margaret fitted easily into the pattern demanded by Dave's parents and saw that he got to work on time. Saturday was the busiest day. His headaches were a problem, but he was a loving father and did all the gardening himself. They made love a lot in the early years.

Dave in no way led her to suspect that he had become actively homosexual. The first thing she knew was when she opened a brown envelope addressed to Dave that looked as if it were some routine local government notice. It was a court receipt for payment of a fine. The date was a day when Dave had taken the day off work to go to hospital for some tests about his headaches. She rang Dave at the cleaner's. 'You weren't at the hospital that day,' she said. 'What is this court receipt for?'

Dave answered by fleeing. He went to his friend's flat, telephoned Margaret from there and told her he was homosexual. 'I don't care what you are,' she said. 'Just come home.'

Margaret told Dave's parents immediately – automatically. That was the kind of family they were. His mother had never dreamed that he was homosexual, although his father had had his suspicions. His father had an influential friend who was a psychiatrist and arranged for Dave to see him. The doctor gave Dave hormones, which had a surprising physical effect. Dave grew breasts. For a long time he wouldn't go swimming and he loves swimming. Finally he stopped taking the pills. They had just taken away his sex drive altogether.

Dave's family thought he was cured – the incident was past history. For a few years, Margaret believed it too, although she noticed times when Dave would come in very late and there were stretches in which he was less interested in sex. Then when, on a holiday without the children – the ideal time, she thought, for getting your sex life back on the rails – he refused to make love the whole week, she realized with a heavy heart that he must have started up with men again.

As they talked, swiftly the two wives perceived their mutual advantages of their husbands' love affair. When their men were out, they knew with whom, and where (at the flat of George's gay friend, who worked late hours and let George and Dave have their own key.)

Together the two women could try and fathom homosexuality. Is it a stronger drive than heterosexuality, they asked each other? They discussed the aspects of homosexuality that they didn't like – the public toilets and the danger of infection, and how out of character it all seemed for the men that they had married. They avoided, then and later, any speculation about whatever their husbands did in bed. Speaking for them both, as she came to do, Lucy concludes

38

that she and Margaret had failed to fathom the urge that could be so great as to drive the men out of the family. 'We agreed that it must be strong because George and Dave would not have done it unless it was so much a part of themselves that it could not be denied. We agreed that we had to learn to love that half of our husbands, because it was part of the whole.'

The two couples determined to try and meet once a month. They negotiated two meetings a week for Dave and George – on Monday and Thursday evenings and, as before, Sunday mornings. Occasionally they would all take the children and go on an outing. On Lucy's birthday they went as a foursome for a Chinese meal.

What to tell the children occupies a lot of their conversation. Dave and Margaret's are older. Dave says the children don't know, but the other three wonder. Dave's sixteen-year-old son gets into a rage if anybody mentions queers. The boy has plenty of girlfriends so his parents don't think he will be a homosexual. One thing that none of Dave's teenage children can stand is his wearing a shoulder bag. He picked up an airline bag when he was on holiday (he managed a few days away with George) and now uses it whenever he goes out. 'Mum,' the children shout, 'does Daddy have to wear that shoulder bag?'

George and Lucy are watching carefully. Perhaps they will wait until their own start asking questions or perhaps they should plan on a formal announcement when the children reach adolescence. Perhaps they will say nothing. Their terror is that some other children might suspect, or learn. Children can be so cruel; what if they shouted, 'Your father's a fairy!'

Thinking about his son's future, George often asks himself what causes homosexuality. He himself was brought up dominated by women; his father died when he was four, not his own son's situation. If Jimmy were gay, George says he would not mind, as long as Jimmy were happy, but he would prefer Jimmy to be straight.

For the time being their fragile quartet is working. Yet both wives have a terror of what could follow the end of the affair, which could come at any time. For example, one evening Lucy walked into their living-room and found George in floods of tears. Dave had been suffering terrible guilt because Margaret had berated him for what he was doing to his family. He had told George that he could not lead a double life any more and that they would have to finish things off. George then broke down. He didn't see how he could live without Dave.

Lucy intervened. She rang Margaret, who had known nothing about the men's quarrel. 'Look,' Lucy said. 'I know George is going to go up to the flat on Sunday morning, in the hope that Dave will be there. Can you sort of pretend to Dave that I need the book I lent him and tell him to bring it up to the flat to give to George?' The ruse worked. Dave had been looking for an excuse to see George and the two men were reconciled.

It can be no more than a day-to-day truce, however. To Lucy, the future is one big question mark. 'I no longer anticipate having an old age with George at all. I know that George and Dave have got a lovely fantasy of life together as a couple, when family commitments lessen, but that might be a straw for them to grasp, to stay together.'

Divorce is something she does not anticipate. 'George loves the children and I know he is responsible enough to stay with them. But when they grow up ... who knows what will happen? I am a lot happier than when I first found out, when I felt my whole marriage had caved in. Now I realize that there is no such thing as security in life – the only security you have is within yourself.'

For George's part, he passionately wants to set up home with Dave. That is really why he had been so upset. The visiting rights that the wives permit, he knows, might sound more than fair for someone who is married and has commitments to his young family: 'But for me, it's not enough; for both of us, it's not enough. The rationed moments are too tense. When we are together, it is always a prearranged thing. I would like just to be with Dave in an ordinary situation. Dave has to work every Saturday and he can hardly ever get a night away. On the Thursday before

Easter last year, we went away to a caravan that Dave has. It was wonderful but so brief and sad. Friday night came and Dave had to go back.

'If I did go off and live with Dave, I find it very difficult to imagine that Lucy and I would never see each other again. We are still attached to each other. I really don't know how I'd feel if she went off with another man. I don't know if the experience I have with Dave is attainable for her. I don't know what she wants from our relationship.'

One nagging doubt for George concerns Dave's continuing sex life with Margaret . . . 'We don't discuss it. I didn't really know until the other week that they were still having a relationship. I know that they did at the beginning, and that it did sort of fade out. Margaret got very upset. "You don't even put your arms around me any more," she said, and that was what she missed most of all. I think that's the trouble with both myself and Dave – we feel that the minute you've made physical contact with your wives, they expect you to go the whole way. Lucy has told me that she'd be quite happy with a cuddle.'

George clings to his dream but what kind of alternative life is there for a man who keeps his children's photos in his wallet, showing them to anyone who would look and whose mother lives down the street and expects her son to bring the grandchildren for tea every Sunday afternoon? His bluff was called when he inherited some money from an uncle. He realized that he had to spend it on an extension to the house. Lucy needed a place for the washing machine, and to change the children when they came in from the garden. 'There goes my chance for a life with Dave,' he said to himself, but he had no choice: 'Once the children are here, you can't look back. They have their personalities. They are your children.'

Margaret's terror is more focused. She lives in a house that shouts that it has nothing to hide. The neatest, best-kept garden in the neighbourhood, shrubs planted like curtains at the side so that the smooth manicured grass leads the eye to the spotless picture window that looks straight through a

41

picture window at the back, revealing more very tidy borders, not a leaf out of place. Margaret has thrown herself into her home, which gleams from every corner, and her children are getting ready to leave. If Dave should depart too, she would have nothing. She's going to hold on. What is on her side is Dave's bondage to his family. Between his family and his job, he is so restricted, that if she were analytical, which she is not, she might consider that his homosexuality is not an urge but a protest, his only possible expression of freedom.

Of the four Dave is the least introspective and the bluntest. He started his homosexual life one night after their first child was born: 'I hadn't had a row with Margaret. That would have been easier, made me feel less guilty. I just went out looking. It was like a hunt. It was exciting. I went into a public toilet and sat down in a booth and waited. There were slits in the walls, for cleaning or something, I suppose, and suddenly a hand came through the wall. I know it sounds sordid to others, meeting people in lavatories, but they could not know what nice people I've met – a professor, no less, and two theatre producers. I've always admired educated people, not being educated myself.

'Margaret might never have known if I had not got arrested. She wouldn't even have known that, because it was in a town about twenty miles from here with a different court. The policeman who caught us was quite nice – but it was in the open air, in the park, clearly illegal – and he said we'd have to appear in court. I had it all managed. I'd got the afternoon off, and no one recognized me in court. Although the news was put in the local newspaper, not only was it in a different area but my name and address were spelled wrong. I've always thought that was the policeman trying to help. Nobody I knew saw it. But' – Dave smacks his head – 'the court sent a receipt for the fine!

'Even though I went to my friend's flat, I stayed away only one night. It was the first night Margaret and I had been apart since we were married. The next morning I went home. I couldn't stand the silence. I missed my children.

'If I were young now, I would never marry. I suppose I'm bisexual, because I've got four children, but I like men. I have no problem in being a homosexual, no problem at all. The problem is hurting people. I would advise any woman whose husband is homosexual to get a divorce. As for the man, if he can make a clean break and not hurt anybody, he's lucky.'

4

Husbands, for Better or Worse

Now that the oppression of homosexuals has lifted slightly and there is a clear alternative way of life, the gay movement and many of its observers theorize that young homosexuals will not be tempted in the future into the heterosexual mould and into marriage. Only time will tell but the prediction itself is the kind of sweeping generalization about homosexuality that is out of date. It ignores the enormous variety and shadings of homosexual behaviour which can manifest itself virtually at any time of life, and with every degree of intensity from total commitment to casual indifference. To say that homosexuals will stop marrying is like saying that all homosexuals have limp wrists. Some will; some do, but others will not and do not.

Anyone who thinks that homosexuals marrying heterosexuals is a thing of the past should talk to Tony. He is a young Cypriot and he lives at home in London with his mother, sisters and brothers. He is an active homosexual. (Active? Several pickups at lunchtime, out to Hampstead Heath, and back to the same pub in the evening for more.) He had been trying over-indulgence as a cure. It did not work. He is looking for a wife.

'Of course, I want to get married. It's the only way to live. What could be drearier than the gay lifestyle? My mother will find me a wife. No, I won't tell the girl I'm gay. Why should I? Cypriot men have never told their wives what they do outside the home. Lots of them have been gay. Anyway I want children. If she's a sympathetic girl, a warm girl, I'm sure I'll be able to perform.'

It is easy to make a list of reasons why homosexual men marry: to conceal their homosexuality, to cure it, to have children, to have a wife, to help out a friend (Somerset Maugham even obliged the importunate Syrie by providing her with a child before the marriage), to get rich, to get a better job. Homosexuals also, like Oscar Wilde, marry out of love: 'The air is full of the music of your voice, my soul and body seem no longer mine, but mingled in some exquisite ecstasy with yours. I feel incomplete without you,' he wrote to Constance Wilde when they were separated briefly during the first year of their marriage in 1884. All of these motives are timeless and will endure, no matter how open and accepted the homosexual way of life becomes.

In preparing their Kinsey Institute study of San Francisco homosexuals for publication in 1978, the authors Alan Bell and Martin Weinberg had to consider how much attitudes towards homosexuality had changed in the eight years since their interviews in 1970. For example, they had detected that one-third of all homosexuals had been married at some time. Yet may not marrying be interpreted as a homosexual expression of anti-homosexuality and self-hatred? Would research later in the decade have detected a lower incidence of marriage? Bell and Weinberg finally decided that any person's acceptance of his or her own means of sexual expression is determined by a complex set of circumstances, among which personal experience and education are equally as important as social climate. As they could see that, despite changing moral standards, homosexuals continued to differ in attitudes towards homosexuality, they concluded that it was reasonable to suppose that what people told them in 1970 was still valid in 1978.

Their main finding, much publicized and a contribution to the death of the stereotype, was that homosexuals are no more neurotic or maladjusted than heterosexuals. Neither, they learned, is there discernible any such thing as one common gay lifestyle. There seem to be at least five types of homosexual. Some are 'close-coupled', as good as married; others are 'open-coupled', combining a steady relationship with casual contacts. A third type are 'functional' – single, very active sexually. The last two function poorly as homosexuals and have virtually no sex life at all.

Bell and Weinberg also confirmed that often homosexuality is one of the secrets men keep from women. Among their

45

homosexual male subjects who had been married, a full two-thirds had not told their wives about their homosexuality before the marriage. To judge from sexual performance, the wives would have had no grounds for suspicion during the first year (unless they were married to one of the 9 per cent who reported wanting no intercourse at all). The majority of the homosexual husbands bounced along in the first year well up to the norm for heterosexual newlyweds, who, according to the control group, had intercourse two to six times a week. What the wives of homosexuals could not know was that 40 per cent of their men were pretending, at one time or another, that they were in bed with a man.

These marriages did not last. Most ended in divorce or separation after a period of three years. Of those men who did give advance warning of their homosexual interests, most promised that after marriage they would give it up. They did not. The observed pattern was remarkably similar to that of George and Lucy and Dave and Margaret. After the birth of the first child, sex faded out of the marriage and homosexuality wafted in, for the husband. The wife turned into a mother. Most of those who had married had produced a child before the marriage fell apart.

If any single motive for marrying should disappear as a result of gay liberation, it is marrying as a cure. As doctors, clergymen and parents gain greater understanding that homosexuality is a constant ingredient in a population mix, and constitutes a force as unstoppable as the heterosexual drive, they cannot help but hesitate these days before advising young men troubled by homosexual thoughts to find a nice girl and settle down. (A pamphlet prepared by the Roman Catholic Social Welfare Commission at the request of Catholic bishops of England and Wales specifically instructs priests not to suggest marriage in those cases.) Yet no amount of public awareness and publicity will stop some young men and women seeking a marriage to ward off homosexual tendencies and to direct their behaviour into the sexual channel into which they hope their sexual desires will flow.

Bob is a Liverpudlian who makes a bawdy tale of his long

efforts, which included marriage and fatherhood, to help 'it to clear up', before deciding to become an all-out gay. Yet he insists, and apparently believes, that he would never have become homosexual if his wife had not left him. The failure of his marriage still hurts him, an insult and reproach to his manhood, all the more wounding because he is a big man, and strong. Although he lives with a lover, he is convinced his gayness does not show. He regrets that he cannot re-create the family life he has left behind for the sake of the child who comes to visit on weekends.

'My wife is now married to her ex-boyfriend. This is going to sound complicated. She hadn't seen him for years. Then when her father died, the twit turned up for the funeral. The moment they looked at each other, I thought, "Here we go." If he hadn't turned up, I'd still be married. My gay self has come up just because I was separated. It had never come out in our marriage, no dirty books, nothing.

'I was a virgin when I married. I had never masturbated or had wet dreams. I only thought it was for urinating out of. (Except there was a coloured girl who seduced me at twelve or thirteen.) We had a big white wedding, in a big church, with a big reception at an hotel.

'When I was ten years old, I suspected I was gay. I looked it up in books. "Oh, it's natural," they said. "It will clear up at around fourteen years of age." So I put it to one side. It got worse at comprehensive school. Two of the rough ones tried to debag me, as I believe it is called. I threw the two of them back. "This is quite easy," I said to myself. I turned to martial arts. "What's a queer like you doing in a sport like this?" they asked me.

'All I thought was that I didn't want to be queer. I didn't want to carry an 'andbag. I was not attracted to little children. I didn't want to wear makeup; it doesn't suit me. I wasn't interested in midnight flashing. I have quite strong willpower and so I put it into the back of my mind. I did some more research and saw that it could go until twenty-two and then it would definitely clear up.

'Now I know that was ridiculous. I've had a boyfriend of

47

fifteen – as big as me. After I was married, I bought a magazine with its gay ads and I went scarlet. "My God," I thought. "It's not going to clear up."

'I'm divorced now. I like girls. I love girls. I married one. But I'm not bisexual. Definitely not.

'I saw the ads for gay pubs. I thought, "Are you or aren't you? Make your mind up." So I went to a pub in Kensington and asked the bartender what a good drink was. I knew nothing about drinking. I had four vodkas and tonics. I began my own pub crawl. I now know I picked the wrong pub . . . my God, it was the real dregs of the gay world, the clothes, the evening gowns.

'I went outside. I was going to be sick. I was molested by this bloke. "Come with me," he said. "No, I'm going home to the wife," I said. "Not if you're in that pub, you're not," he said. We went into that little park by the church there. What he was telling me to do, in his own little gay slang (I didn't understand a word of it) . . . it sounded very rude. "You've got to take all your clothes off!" I said. "I don't want to do that." I looked and there he was standing stark naked, in the cemetery. "Are you ready?" I says. He says yes. "Then turn around!" I says. He turned around, and I said, "By-eee." And I took off and didn't stop running till I was at Victoria.

'I was working for the council at that time. There was this guy Simon that worked with me in the office had beautiful eyes. I had been separated for about four months. I gave a party. I always had girls there; people stayed until 3 a.m. Then most went home. Simon says to me, "Everybody else has somewhere to sleep, and I don't. Mind if I have the other half of your bed?" "All right," I says. First thing I knew, it was arm over, leg over . . . Well, what he wanted, happened. A good old-fashioned grope. None of this anal sex. None of this oral sex. If he had tried anal sex, I would have smashed him across the room.

'Monday morning. Back at the office. I go in. "Morning, girls! Morning, lads!" No answer. Then a snigger. He had *told*. That night, this girl Louise who was a friend of mine came round the pub with me. "What's this about you and

Simon?" she says. "You seduced him while he was asleep! You turned him over and raped him! He says you split his arse and there was blood all over the sheets, and he had to go and sleep on the settee!"

'I said, "That's a lie. The very opposite of what happened. He tried to rape *me*!"

'"I knew you'd never do a thing like that, Bob," she said.

'"Thanks, Louise," I said.

'A week later nobody was speaking to Simon. Because he was a liar. And bisexual.'

Bob decided to find his own style of being gay. He found a pub in Vauxhall where everybody looked like 'ordinary blokes' – even the females; ('they also looked like ordinary blokes') and where they talked about football. He found a fellow who became his 'affair' and who taught him the theory and the language of being gay – the 'parlary', they call it. 'Varda means look. Cods is what's between a man's legs. Dish is a backside. Omo is a man. Bonomo is a good-looking man. So you could say in a straight pub, "Varda the dish on that omo" and nobody else would know what you was talking about.

'Then I had to make a choice between bitch or macho (butch). I got mixed up. The bloke who was teaching me was butch – but effeminate. My own fancy is nice sweet boys, about twenty, petit blonds, but I also can fancy very butch tough boys. I tried both. In the end I had to make up my mind. I didn't want to wear all the frilly bits. I went in for the James Dean look, collar up. I went in for the leather jacket, T-shirt and plimsolls. I also tried oral sex. I was good at it. I must say, in the group I went around in, I was known as a master.

'Now I am settled. I have an affair who I've been living with for about a year. We don't have anal intercourse. It hurts and I don't like it. (I can be the active one at times, but you don't have to be either. You can use other parts.) My boy, he likes to be active, but I say, "Get off! I can't stand anymore!" and we stop straightaway. The problem is that sexually, we're both butch. The butch ones that pick you up will say, "Anybody can change." "Not me, buster,"

I say, and they stay away – me with my 38-inch chest which I once got up to 43 inches.

'My affair and I, we don't have a full sex thing, but we love each other. Are we faithful? Well, he won't find out, will he? To some men, it is a real stigma that I've slept with a woman. I could go to bed with a woman now. As an ordinary feat of sexual acrobatics. You can't be bisexual without emotional pleasure. My boy and I, our sex life is nothing but mutual masturbation – unless I can get to sleep first.'

Bob believes that nobody outside the gay world knows of his homosexuality. He is also a proud father and likes, in gay bars, to mention his daughter.

'I have access to her. I see her every two weeks. I pick her up and she stays with me and Dick. I've explained to her, "He lives so far away, he just has to stay the weekend." During the visits, my daughter sleeps in my double bed with me, and Dick sleeps on the settee. My daughter – she's sharp even though she's only six – has actually asked me, do Dick and I sleep together.

' "He sleeps on the settee," I say.

' "What about when I'm not here?" she asks.

'Now I may be digging a hole for myself but I told her, "Men don't sleep in the same bed together. Only men and women sleep together."

'My parents I've never told. My father's a milkman. What would it do to my father to hear that his big butch son, who's his favourite child and become everything he wasn't, was a queer?

'What about getting older? I worry about that. I've been to see a plastic surgeon about removing some acne scars. My prematurely grey hair is hereditary. I plan to start tinting it. As for wrinkles, I'm all right until about forty-five. My legs are all right, although I had a cartilage taken out for an old injury. Not football. Disco dancing.'

To tell or not to tell? For the still-married homosexuals, it is the most burning question of their lives. Most resolve it in favour of silence. Most cities in North America and Europe now have gay switchboards. These counselling services are

50

accustomed to poignant calls from married gays. The London Gay Switchboard makes an estimate in line with the Kinsey Institute Study's that only about 10 per cent tell their wives. Typical is the man, married for twenty-five years, whose gay sex life has been wordless sex usually in public lavatories, and who says over the line: 'You're the first gay person I've ever spoken to.' It has taken a lot of courage for him to make the first call. (Even so, some men do it with the imperiousness of someone who has at last made up his mind to buy a Mercedes: 'I'm a married man. I have no intention of telling my wife, but I would like to meet gay men. Preferably someone in the eighteen to twenty-four age group, and blond.' The caller is probably over forty-five and bald.) The switchboard never arranges meetings but will give out the addresses of gay clubs and organizations, some of which cater for 'new' gays.

Telling – 'coming out' – is no easy single step even for the bachelor homosexual. To whom do you come out – just to one person, to all your friends, to your family (brothers and sisters, or parents as well), people at work, the whole world? Telling usually follows months or years of hesitation, but for the married homosexual, as husband after husband repeats, what is told cannot be untold.

'The psychiatrist suggested I tell my wife, then pack my things and move out,' said a London hospital porter. 'One night I broke down and told her. Her first reaction was, "I can take it." The second night I was sleeping on the floor. She said if it was another woman, she could cope. But a man made her feel sick. She said if I was prepared to give up a homosexual existence, we could carry on as before. Me being the jerk that I am, I agreed. I don't think it's going to work. As soon as homosexuality is mentioned on television, off goes the set. One of the conditions she made is that I don't buy *Gay News* and that I don't associate with any gay people. If I go anywhere, she wants to know where you've been. She opens my letters. The children know. It doesn't make the slightest bit of difference to them. But my mother doesn't know. My wife uses that as a threat. Yes, that's why I'm still at home.'

51

Many homosexuals elect secrecy because they believe their marriage would not survive revelation, and they want to stay married. One whose name could well be Lionel would like to tell his wife and his straightforward, articulate manner makes it seem reasonable that he should do so. In his late fifties, tall, with spectacles, and thick grey hair, he looks like what he is: a successful executive in a Manchester engineering firm with a big staff and big budget. He lives a life finely balanced between security and risk, marriage and homosexuality, fidelity and fun. 'I'm not in constant danger,' he says, 'because I'm not wildly promiscuous. I would lose my job if my gayness were found out, but at the same time I've been active in the homosexual movement because I can make a contribution.' Any gay could turn him in, but none ever threatens to, and the prospect does not weigh on his mind.

He has been gay for only six years, and loves it. He feels healthier, happier, nicer, more relaxed in every way; he is puzzled, in fact, that his wife has not noticed the change in him. 'If I told Jane, it might lessen her respect for me. She's always very caustic when homosexuality is mentioned. Her respect is based on qualities she knows I've got. It's dishonest, of course, not telling her, and I am bothered about that. I haven't thought of telling either of my two grown-up daughters because I don't know how they'd take it.'

How long can he expect the double life to continue, having a private homosexual world and a stable marriage to Jane?

'I haven't thought of that not being the case. Life has been tougher for Jane. She's been saddled with a much tougher temperament. She was very fond of her father. He was, she says, the only person who *really* understood her; they were akin, with mercurial temperaments. I never felt she got much fun out of life. She derived her satisfaction from books.

'There is no problem making time for homosexuality. The nature of my job is night committee meetings. One or two more aren't noticeable. An afternoon in bed with somebody is always possible. My current friend, we go to

52

his place when his wife's away or we go to our cottage in the Lake District. Or hotels. Some of my gay friends have flats.'

A woman cannot help but observe how male male homosexuals are! With what confidence and ease they can manage two lives: Lionel says 'an afternoon in bed with somebody is always possible' with the same executive air in which he states, 'I control a budget of three million a year.'

His life with Jane is definitely not one of quiet desperation. When they go out to dinner, Lionel says, people are aware of them as an interesting couple. 'We complement each other. People are sometimes astonished at us. We were both at university at the same time, but she's brighter than me. She works as a part-time textbook editor. At home in the evening, we get out the gin and tonic and sit on the terrace and talk over the day.

'There was not much sex activity between us ever. She never seemed to enjoy it. I'm far more successful sexually with men than with women. I had a very puritanical upbringing. I was hung up enough never to experiment. I wouldn't mind if Jane would find somebody who could liberate her sexually. It would be very wholesome. A woman, even. I wouldn't mind.

'Where was homosexuality the first fifty years of my life? Some fantasies, yes, in adolescence, but nothing came of it. I wasn't fighting it back in adult life. I just never thought about it. I'm not looking for the great homosexual love, no. It just hasn't happened. I feel very lucky. I've got a super family and the bonus of having satisfactory sex outlets as well.'

Lionel and Jane, to be sure, married just after the war. It was as unlikely then that a homosexual would tell his wife as it was in the middle ages. However, it is easy to exaggerate the effect of the recent sexual revolution on individual lives. Plenty of young men are going to the altar or registry office with their secret intact. The real question is whether they have told themselves.

An American sociologist, Brian Miller, who has studied the living patterns of American gay fathers, distinguishes between those like Lionel, who have not told their wives but are 'out' to their own gay circle, and 'trade' fathers, men who have scarcely admitted the truth to themselves.

A thin, straw-haired young man of thirty-one, who is so afraid of being identified that he will not say what city he comes from or what job he does, described the agony of a double life – but not before pulling out a colour photograph of himself, the wife and kids on the beach. He is struggling to explain to himself what is going on in his life: 'I didn't have many girlfriends as a teenager. When I met my wife, it seemed like a normal relationship. We thought a lot of each other but didn't want a premarital pregnancy, so we didn't sleep together. I felt I was in love. We got engaged a year after we met; two years later we were married. We were saving very seriously during that time. I hid all my homosexual feelings. Two years later when we had a child, our sex life deteriorated. Then I found as well as sex two or three times a week with my wife, I felt I needed a top-up. But it had to be a male top-up. It improved our sex life together but she doesn't know. If she did find out, I'd feel so ashamed, and bad. I don't know if I could make love to her again. I don't know if she'd want me.

'If I had known I was gay, I might not have married. I've hidden behind marriage, getting married to convince myself I wasn't gay. Everybody thinks homosexuals are nasty and degrading, and now I know that they're not. Married gays go to the toilets – it's very dodgy with the police. They're afraid to go to gay bars. They're afraid of queer-bashers. You think you've got a friend – and then they beat you up. And if somebody saw me from work, I'd be out of my job certainly, I'd be sunk.

'Now I've met this friend, and at first we got together in a cubicle and masturbated and talked. "Don't keep talking . . . in here," he said. We went back to his place in my car. "Are you married?" he said. "You've got children, haven't you?" He'd seen the child's car seat. I've allowed him anal intercourse – I'd never been quite willing to go that far. But I wanted to experiment, to get something more out of life. I've come to trust him. I'd better. He has my home phone number. He could ruin my whole marriage.

54

'Before him I had another relationship, with a very young person. I was looking for someone young. I met him at the toilets – it's a terrible double life I lead. I cry about it sometimes. "Can I see you again?" I asked. Then I found out he was sixteen. He looked twenty, one of my own generation. He was a public-school boy. It got too dangerous; there were only two cubicles there. We would meet in alleys and then I would walk him back to school, to make sure he was safe. He had to be back by half-past five.

'Then one day he said, "I usually want money for this." I had no faith in him anymore. He would toss a man off for 50p or a packet of cigarettes. I didn't want that. I wanted fulfilment sexually. But my heart was too involved. I had fallen in love with him. My wife, my marriage, my work were all in danger. In the rain, when it was snowing, I would walk round and round to see if I could find him. I'd go to the toilet and he wouldn't be there. I would see him with friends and he would ignore me. One night I was in such a state that I didn't want to go home. I was lost, distraught, so hurt that I wrote a poem about him.

'I had told him I was married. "That's all right," he said. "I want to get married some day." But he stopped seeing me.

'My new gay friend is older, we have a lot in common, we like sports and jogging. But it's breaking up. We had a long talk the other night. He said, "William, we've got to cool it. I'm falling in love with you. After I saw you with your children, I realized how much you love them. Although I know you're totally gay, I knew I could not do that to you and to them and to the wife. Say you tell your wife you're gay. You're going to break up your home; you've got a mortgage and commitments. You wouldn't be able to afford my kind of life. You're being selfish, William. You want your cake and eat it too. You've got to go back to your wife."

'But I've got to have somebody gay to talk to. It was a man-to-man thing that night, no sex, just a talk. He's not effeminate. Neither am I. Just two normal men, that's all.'

*

55

Most married homosexuals maintain silence because they think they would lose everything – their wife, their family, and their job, if their secret became public. Another reason is that there is no need. Many can sustain a double life indefinitely without anxiety, as Lionel proved. Heterosexual adultery on the other hand resolves itself. The Other Woman pulls and pulls and, if the affair continues, the man usually has to choose between the wife and the other woman. Homosexuality often means not choosing but staying in limbo.

The Other Man may find it just as convenient to keep on living his own or double life. He will probably not indulge in feminine tricks, such as calling the lover's wife and saying, 'There's something I think you ought to know.' Yet many homosexuals have no time for secrecy, and this may be a pattern of the future. They love their wives, have told their wives and believe that marriage is a fine institution and that homosexuality as an outlet for extramarital desires is far more accommodating than adultery.

A Massachusetts businessman says that his second marriage was more than pleasant camouflage. 'There was this nice rapport such as I've never had with another human being. She was a tremendous business partner and we shared the upbringing of our daughters. The sort of marriage people are talking about now, we had then, good, exceptionally good.

'In the case of a gay person like me, I was not looking for another relationship. That would have been cheating. If both hets [heterosexuals] are cheating, the chances are that one of them will find a het relationship that takes higher priority. It would have pulled the marriage apart. If I were young now, I would probably marry the second of my two wives again. We had so much to talk about. But today's gays will probably not marry, with today's passion for doing your own thing.

'She was a fine woman. I say "was" because, after twenty-four years of marriage and three children, she died. We had a great deal in common beside chartered surveying, the business that brought us together and which we set up in jointly. Music, books. She was a handsome woman. We discussed my homosexuality and she said it was no problem. Within three or four days of our wedding, I was out having sex with men. I never expected to give it up and wasn't expected to. I simply had to have both.

'We had a very satisfying sex life, on her part and on mine. My extracurricular activity was no deterrent. Sex is sex. I'm strong and healthy. I didn't play roles. In bed, we stuck to a few established patterns but we went at it with enthusiasm.

'When we moved from the city to a small town, I was so busy I didn't have much time for homosexuality. I had to be more careful. Being gay in a small town and being in business is not easy. Being careful means that you don't look at people the way you would in Boston or New York City. You don't cruise; you aren't seen in the wrong places. You have to go to other towns. I had business in fifteen other towns within a fifty-mile radius, so opportunities arose there.

'Do I miss female sex? No, not really. I'm a workaholic. I do miss relationships. I wouldn't mind having one. At my age, it's not likely, although I know I should be proud to be healthy, active and looking this attractive. I'm somewhat promiscuous and somewhat into anonymous sex. At night, if I've been working late, which is usually, I go down to the Esplanade. There's mad sex there as soon as the sun has gone down. You can get anything you want. In spite of the MBTA police. If you are careful enough to watch you won't be caught. I find outdoor sex to be exciting, and relatively safe. I keep to the Esplanade. The Fenway is much more dangerous.'

In the closet or out, most homosexuals interviewed for this book declared frankly that one of their reasons for marrying was the desire for children. For some it was their only reason. They gritted their teeth and went through with it. A man who is an import-exporter, gay since the age of nine, admits that he loathed heterosexual intercourse, when he first tried it in the Merchant Marines: 'The Boy Virgin, they called me. At the instigation of the chief mate I'd been

57

sleeping with, they took me to a prostitute in Panama. I had been expecting all sorts of bells to ring and they didn't. I had trouble getting an erection. I told the girl, "I need some help!" Eventually I managed it. Did I feel dirty afterwards! I fled back to the ship and to somebody's bunk and made wild love to get the girl out of my system.'

But when he met a woman engineer who was a lesbian, they both decided to try to go straight. 'I desperately loved children and I knew the non-normal would not produce children and the normal would.' The reproduction worked; the marriage did not. Today, the father of four, he is divorced and living with a lover in a homosexual milieu. He hopes his boys will grow up bisexual. 'Then they'll have the best of both worlds, but the girls . . . I think that any girl who even suspects that her boyfriend is homosexual should run in the opposite direction. They make terrible husbands. Nobody has ever abandoned homosexuality because of marriage in my experience. Nobody. They always revert to it. It *is* stronger.'

There are publicly acknowledged homosexuals who marry more than once and given the right woman would do it again. A woman is a better wife, so to speak, than a man. Those of this persuasion interviewed for this book insisted that they were excellent lovers for their wives.

'*Everybody* knows, love. My daughter knows. My son knows. My wife knew before we were engaged, and that was in 1942, when it mattered. I knew I was bisexual since I was seven. I knew I had a very strong attraction to my own sex. I always wanted to marry. I *always* wanted children. My two older brothers, both killed in the war, married very young. I always wanted to be like my brothers.

'Marrying, in my mind, was something one had to do. In my teens, I discovered I could fuck women. (I was an Eton-Balliol type. It went round the school that I used to tear up to Cork Street and have women at £3 a time.) Yet a homosexual love affair went right through my schooldays. Three years, totally secret – a single love at Eton – yes, it's possible.

'I met a musician. I was never in love with her but she was an attractive, vivacious girl, with tremendous guts. She fell in love with me. "I think you ought to know I'm bisexual," I told her. She had never heard of it. Together we went to a psychiatrist. He was breezy – "just an adolescent phase", he said. She excused my infidelity and we married.

'My wife had to take an awful lot, but we had a perfectly satisfactory sex relationship. It was never from my gut, it was something I did because I was fond of her, because she had a normal sexual appetite. At the end of our marriage, about ten years ago, she said I had given her the most perfectly satisfying sex life she could have wanted. She did have one extramarital affair. It was a complete failure. "That showed me what you are like as a lover," she said. But from my point of view, sexual intercourse with her was performed out of tenderness, plus a strong desire to please, and duty.

'We had two children, and lots of misfortunes connected with childbearing – a fallopian pregnancy, a false pregnancy, two miscarriages – and then a girl and a boy. I absolutely adored being a father. I have the happiest memories of my children's childhood.

'I have quite a strong longing to be married again. My daughter is putting me in the way of likely ladies and this friend I mentioned . . . she's in her middle forties and I half-feel I want to develop it. Now, however, I'm frightened: can I sexually relate to a woman? Perhaps nine years of living as a homosexual has spoiled me. Why do I want to remarry? I like solitude, but I don't like loneliness. My life would be fuller and happier if there were a solid relationship which was going on. I like the idea of living with somebody even if it is not coming back every evening to slippers warmed. It is hard to achieve this with a man. I have tried. I fell in love in 1970. That's what broke up my marriage. My wife couldn't accept a marriage with no sex. She couldn't agree to separate rooms – my suggestion.

'This man and I are still close friends. I see him every third day. But no sex now between us for seven years. He has violent mood swings. He too wants to marry. He is constantly flirting with marrying. I think there is something non-complementary about two men living together. I can't go out in the streets to say "Gay is Beautiful". Gay is Bloody.

'Perhaps Mr Right is just around the corner, but surely it's not conceivable. As Quentin Crisp asks of all these homosexuals looking for the dark stranger, "But is the dark stranger looking for you?" The homosexual, in 99 cases out of 100, gives himself no chance for lasting relationships. He trains himself to get his kicks from one-night stands.'

To many overt homosexuals, such longings after family life are sentimental and meretricious. If they ever blundered into marriage, they were relieved when they sloughed it off. To them, a home and fidelity are bourgeois chains that they have thrown off, one of the best things about being gay. The family is dead, decadent or dying.

In *Dancer from the Dance*, Andrew Holleran's tragi-comic novel of gay life in Manhattan, the hero is a beautiful young man named Malone. He looks like a Greek god and seeks perfect love in an endless quest through gay discos from the Bowery to Fire Island. Yet he moans constantly for what is forever beyond his reach. 'I want to live in a big white house and sit on my porch and see fireflies blinking in the evening, and smell burning leaves in the fall, and see my children playing on the lawn . . .' His best friend, a drag queen named Sutherland, is contemptuous. No visions of domestic bliss spoil his days. 'Children require a womb,' said Sutherland, 'and a womb is connected to a vagina, and the thought of cooze makes you vomit. Such a small detail . . .'

Dr Bruce Voeller, founder of the American National Gay Task Force, thinks that homosexuals like himself will not marry in the future because they will be aware, as he was not while growing up, that there were 'esteemable people who are homosexuals'. He thinks that the wish for children has been part of social conditioning, equating sex with procreation. Also he believes that in the future (as will be discussed in Chapter 9) there may be gay alternatives for fathering for those homosexual men, probably a minority, but a substantial one, who passionately want to be parents.

His own early experience, Dr Voeller hopes, is becoming an anachronism. When he was fourteen or fifteen, he went to his minister in a small town in Oregon, and told him he thought he was homosexual. The minister was outraged; how could a star athlete and student be one of those vile people? Later at college, a psychiatrist gave him the same angry pep-talk in a more sophisticated version. As a result Voeller married, had three children and was five years into a marriage which lasted eleven years before he realized that he was living a lie, that he had been misled, that he had been brainwashed.

Divorced men living in a totally gay world look back with disbelief at their past as husbands. The bridegroom of Chapter 1 has lived for many years with his lover, a man, who has been exclusively homosexual for as far back as he can remember and who likes to joke that he's 'never even seen one'.

The argument is sometimes made that married homosexuals are afraid of the gay world and loathe it because all they know of it is the clandestine impersonal homosexual underground. 'As long as they remain marginal to the gay world, their ability to achieve safe, fulfilling homosexual relationships remains minimal', Brian Miller declared, in a paper called 'Unpromised Paternity', presented to the American Sociological Association.

If this thesis is true, the obvious implication is that when men enter the gay world fully, they ought to give up impersonal sex and begin to establish close relationships. Yet the experience of some of the men quoted in this chapter belies this expectation. They have been fully gay for years and are either seeking anonymous sex, or a new marriage. But they are older men who may have been conditioned by their past and who, in any case, do not claim to speak for anybody but themselves.

5

The Understanding Wife

The shock of the wife who discovers that her husband is homosexual has no parallel among the female traumas. While it is no more novel than any of the others, still she feels utterly desolate, the first woman in history to whom it has happened. It usually comes as a bombshell, often as not from a husband who has been steadying himself for months or years to deliver it. There are no old wives' tales to prepare her; no traditional jokes ('Who was that lady I saw you with last night?') or clues like lipstick stains to warn her from girlhood that homosexuality, like adultery, is something a wife should be on the look-out for. When the news comes, she does not tell her best friend, her sister or her mother.

For the wife who finds out about the Other Woman, a common reaction is to fight back, female to female. She loses a stone, changes her hairstyle, buys new clothes and tries to recapture her man. Often she seeks out the rival and fights, literally, or rings up in the middle of the night. Whatever her tactic, she does not need imagination: there is plenty in the cultural storechest.

How do you fight another man? That is the lyric cry of gays' wives. Not by being sexy; that is what drove him off in the first place. One young wife says that when she first learned the truth, 'I felt I couldn't look at my body. I felt it had been a letdown to me. I couldn't curl my hair or wear pretty things. Nothing was going to make any difference.' Another wife described the feeling of rejection as going beyond defeminization, to her entire self: 'I realized that I could not *be* the right person for him.'

The suspicion grows that she was not woman enough to get a real man in the first place. (It says something about the male misunderstanding of women that gay husbands totally mistake what the reaction of their wives will be when they are told; it is not rage, not 'Out, you filthy queer!' but rather, 'What is wrong with *me?*') Thus demoralized, usually the last thing she can do is to run out and try to attract another man. The loss of confidence can strike even a woman who is not actually married to her partner; even a woman who is young, blonde and good-looking:

'In the beginning he was good in bed. I was sexually inexperienced but I'd had one other relationship and I knew what fun sex was. When he came along, I thought, Fine, we'll have a good few years. But he's become increasingly homosexual: exclusively now, really, and I've had to adjust. He brings home his guys. Often they ignore me, they're so selfish, wrapped up in themselves. The beautiful body is everything. They don't notice anything, really. He's into blacks now. All his boyfriends are black gays, mostly West Indian. Some stare at me. Sometimes they make *me* feel queer. I feel the abnormal one. They look at me and wonder, "What's that woman doing here?"'

'He, my boyfriend, wants me to have a baby. He doesn't like children, but he wants a baby. Why? If I don't do it, he says he'll find a lesbian mother who wants impregnating. And he tells me that if I get an abortion, I'm getting older and might not be able to have more children.

'Should I leave him? I don't know. We bought this house together. Our parents would be shocked if we broke up. Would a heterosexual man want me now? I wonder.'

Some women make the decision to divorce quite swiftly. Their husbands have become strangers. The marriage has nothing more to offer them and they cut their losses. That is the advice that some family counsellors will offer: make a clean break. One who did, vivacious, red-haired, earning a good salary, regrets only that she did not find out earlier. It was twelve years before the news came out, but she reasons that thirty-six is not such a bad age to be making a fresh start:

'I did *not* make scenes. I did *not* try to get in touch with the other person. He used to ring me when my husband moved back home again experimentally for a while but I asked him to stop. He has asked to meet me and I told my husband I had nothing to say to him.

'When my husband told me he was gay, I can't even remember what he said. My mind is a blank. It was such a shock, like a death. It just blacked everything out. But I'm getting a divorce and determined to remain friends for our son's sake.'

She sounds like the guide to less sure women and to look at her you would believe it. She would believe it too, if she had been able to find a new man for herself. Her confidence has not recovered. 'I'm not taking cold showers or anything like that, but I do keep very busy. I don't know why I can't find any boyfriends. I wouldn't like to break up a home, but I'm no angel. If it happened, I would do it. I seem to have men as friends but they don't seem to turn into lovers. I don't know why. It must be something about me. I think I can spot homosexuals now. I went to a party last weekend and I felt that about three of the fifteen men there were gay. I don't know how I know. It's a blankness when they talk to a woman.'

Temperamentally, however, the wives of homosexuals are poorly suited to walk out of the door. It is no accident that they choose homosexual men as husbands, unwittingly or not. As a type, they tend to be virgins when they marry, or close to it. No critics of performance, but rather nice plain girls, who want a home and children, who are sexually inexperienced and have never wanted sex so much that they could not do without it, and who are prepared to overlook a lot for a nice companionable man who is not trying to jump them. The description of his future wife by the novelist, Evelyn Waugh, a reformed homosexual, illustrates these characteristics. In a letter to Nancy Mitford, Waugh wrote: 'I have taken a great fancy to a young lady named Laura, fair, very pretty, rather long thin nose, very thin and might be dying of consumption to look at her, virgin, Catholic, quiet and astute.' He was not a prepossessing suitor, as his next letter, describing a visit to London to see Laura, indicates: 'I had a hangover and I was sick a good deal on the table, so perhaps that romance is shattered.'

A psychological portrait of this kind of wife appears in *Understanding Women Married to Male Homosexuals* by Dr Myra

S. Hatterer, a New York psychiatrist in a practice with her husband, Dr Lawrence J. Hatterer, specializing in the treatment of homosexuality. She saw women in joint sessions of therapy in which the husbands also participated. She also talked alone to a dozen other wives of homosexuals.

These women, Dr Hatterer observed, were sexually repressed and inhibited, able to put up with long periods of sexual deprivation; they were also inhibited in showing other emotions, like anger. All had had trouble with their fathers, who seemed to be tyrannical and seductive while at the same time ineffectual as males, sometimes bisexual or homosexual themselves. The women felt devalued by their fathers and were hostile towards men without being aware of it. Time and again, they had selected homosexual partners, moving from one to another. They were daughters of women who had low self-esteem and appeared as victims in their own marriages.Most telling, every one of the wives was sexually and socially inexperienced prior to marriage, and saw herself as a failure in competing with other women for men.

The marriages that resulted were, in many cases, neurotic contracts. The men defeminized the wives; the women emasculated their husbands, encouraging their excessive passivity and dependence, while labelling these qualities sensitivity and gentleness. All of the couples welcomed an impoverished sex life at the start. When tensions sprang up it was when one or the other wanted changes, particularly a child. The husbands felt more devalued when they saw the child as a rival for their wives' attention, and their homosexual behaviour increased.

Wives of homosexuals, in other words, are women who when they find a gentle man, one who is not like the others, are glad.

The stoicism shown by these wives can be astonishing. Many decide to try and make it work. That means giving up a sex life of their own but they rarely say that. A farmer's wife says, 'I know I have to be patient because my husband is a very shy person. An extramarital affair for me is out of the question. I am not that sort. I am not going to get a job.

65

We have enough money. We have three children and there's a big house to run. My days are full. Why does this one thing have to intrude? I desperately want him to show me the nice side of homosexuality. The public-toilet side and the court-case side I have seen, but I am gradually building a better image in my mind now that he has come out to me. I don't want a divorce. He is my best friend. Friends are terribly important and I don't want to lose him. It has all happened, after all, through no fault of his own.'

Sigma is a British self-help group for people married to or living with people who are bi- or homosexual. Its major appeal is to wives of homosexuals and although it refrains from giving advice, it tends to attract mainly those wives who want to hold on to their marriages. Its implicit message is that gay-straight marriages can be more open and honest than the conventional kind. 'Many of us,' one of its leaflets reads, 'have been able to re-negotiate our marriage contracts so that both ourselves and our husbands can lead a fuller and happier life in which we can share our concern for each other.'

From time to time, Sigma holds a conference on homosexuality and marriage. At one of these, held at a provincial English university, the group was composed mostly of wives. The gay husbands had stayed at home to look after the children. In the rain, the university looked raw and new. The porter was dubious about the location of the homosexuality conference. The leaders of the conference were either gay-straight couples or homosexuals in pastoral professions – social work, teaching, the church. The workshops covered various topics, but they all quickly got down to the same subject: women wanting to burst out of the closet of their own secret lives. They were no longer inhibited about talking about sex, even over meals. Most, it seemed, still shared double beds.

'Mike caresses me,' said one of the pretty ones. (Some were desperately plain.) 'I get an orgasm. But sometimes I think, "Oh, to have an erect penis inside me!" But that's what he gives to Derek.'

They talked about how they found out: 'He kept bringing this new man from his office home for the weekend, saying that he was lonely, far from his family, and one day I thought, "My God. He's brought his lover home!"' Another arrived home unexpectedly early from a visit to her mother and found her husband in their bed with a man. They debated whether they felt more worried by promiscuity or by a steady affair. One adviser quoted American research suggesting that homosexual love, not homosexual sex, is the real threat to a marriage. Several wives scoffed at the 'If you love me, you'll love this part of me' line. One, bolder than the others, confessed that she threw her husband out and has had a couple of lovers since. She portrayed herself as someone who would not make the same mistake again –'It's not that my husband married his mother when he married me. I married *him* for his mothering characteristics.'

One of the male counsellors listed on his fingers four reasons for staying with his wife: (1) Their marriage is not that much based on sex anyway; (2) they have so many interests and activities in common; (3) 'I happen to be very fond of these two kids we have'; (4) 'Neither of us wants the hassle of splitting up, finding new places to live, dividing everything down the middle, just because of this one strange thing that has come between us.' His wife, a pleasant and intelligent professional woman, almost defiantly sexless, nodded in agreement.

They all discussed the problem that wives face just as much as the husbands – whom to tell and how. 'It would kill my mother' is a defence the group will not accept. One gay counsellor said that before telling, he thought that if it would kill his mother, that was her problem. 'Anybody who is upset by me, how I am, that is their problem, not mine.' When he told both his parents, they did not die but took it very well.

There was little mention of divorce, none of cure. A quiet, slim girl said, 'I just found out two months ago. We've been married for nine years. Our children are a boy, six, and a girl, four. Nobody suggests he can be cured. Oh no. He's not going to change. If he fought it all these years and couldn't hide it, there's no way he's going to hide it now. I don't know what the future holds. Maybe we'll split up. Right now, I'm trying to understand what it is my husband's feeling, and what other wives are feeling. We agreed that if he'd told me five years ago when the children were infants, I probably would have had a complete breakdown.'

The conference spanned a Saturday night and the organizers, for reasons they did not explain, suggested a visit to a gay bar. The wives signed up eagerly and put on their best dresses – a chance to go out on the town and to look at the world their husbands knew so well. In the centre of the city, all concrete and furniture stores, it was obviously Saturday night for heterosexuals. A black man and a blowsy white woman, both drunk, held each other up at a bus stop. Young lovers, hand in hand, gazed through the shop-windows at shiny three-piece suites. Gangs of boys whistled at anything female, even gays' wives. Will homosexuality ever take its place in that street scene?

Down a back street the gay club seemed a refuge. The group relaxed. The bar was uncrowded, utterly ordinary. There was no fancy dress except for one of the counsellors, who had changed for the occasion. He wore a black leather jacket and a leather cap covering his bald spot. He kept both on in spite of the sweat pouring down. There was nothing on the back of the jacket, as he turned to show. 'No nail studs. That would have been a bit obvious.' An iridescent badge on the front proclaimed 'AC–DC'.

The lesbians present were overweight girls who slumped. Gay men, it seems, look after their figures; many lesbians believe that fat is a feminist issue and let theirs go. A sexy-looking girl in an off-the-shoulder black dress was chatting with one of the men at the bar. Which side was she on? The line of wives was explained to the management, who smiled blankly. They sat, print dresses, spectacles, curled hair and make-up, in a row and ordered glasses of beer.

Down in the basement the disco was throbbing. The gay counsellors asked some of the wives to dance – the pretty ones. The dance floor was dark, hot, pulsating – men gyrating in proximity to men but there were women there too and one dreamer was dancing alone. 'It's a man's world', sang the music.

What time to go? Did the men want to be left alone? Most of the wives decided to leave early. 'That music!' said one as she got her coat. 'It surged right through me! I felt completely caught up in it.'

'What a waste,' she added going out the door with the all-female early leavers. 'That's all I could think: All those good-looking young men!'

Over drinks before the last lunch of the conference, one of the gay organizers surveyed the scene. 'Look at these women. In spite of all the pain they've suffered because of their husbands' gayness, they've got a lot of happiness. Look what they're giving to each other. It's lovely to see.'

But were they not taking second-best, selling themselves short? 'Yes, they are. But women seem to think that a cuddle is as good as the real thing.' What these wives needed, he agreed, were ways to meet straight men. Organizations should work towards that goal. 'Even seeing a male choir might help, or visits to discos. But you'd have to be careful not to get men just interested in a quick fuck.'

Many homosexual men, it is obvious, make the ordinary pipe-and-slippers male chauvinist look like a feminist. Many married homosexuals believe fervently in the myth of the understanding wife. 'My lover is married,' many a homosexual man will say, 'but he has an understanding wife.' The understanding is no illusion to be sure, nor the patience nor long suffering; these are all too real. The myth consists in believing that the women do not need sex as much as a man does – a cuddle keeps them happy, and if there are children as well, what more could a woman want?

The myth is no modern concoction. Proust conveyed it beautifully: 'A husband who is that way inclined usually makes his wife happy,' he asserts in 'Time Regained' from *Remembrance of Things Past*.

The young Vicomte de Courvoisier thought he was the only man alive, perhaps the only man since the beginning of the world, to be tempted by someone of his own sex. Supposing this inclination to come to him from the devil, he struggled against it, married an extremely pretty wife and had children by her. Then one of his cousins taught him that the tendency is fairly widespread and was even so kind as to take him to places where he could indulge it. M. de Courvoisier became fonder than ever of his wife and redoubled his philoprogenitive zeal, and he and she were quoted as the happiest couple in Paris.

Ignorance is bliss, in Proust's view. An even more exalted mother figure has to be invented to explain the wife who knows about her husband's homosexuality and smilingly accepts it. This paragon is drawn to perfection by Christopher Isherwood in *A Meeting by the River*. First of all, the main character, an English publisher named Paddy, tells the young lover he is brushing off to think of finding himself a wife:

> If you honestly don't like girls, you don't – all I'm urging is that you should give them a few more tries. They *do* have their advantages, you know, the chief of which is that they can provide you with children. You of all people, with so much love to give, ought not to miss the marvellous experience of being a father. I can promise you that becoming a husband is a very small price to pay for it!
>
> Being married does make a lot of things easier, because the world accepts marriage at its face value, without asking what goes on behind the scenes – whereas it's always a bit suspicious of bachelors! The unmarried are apt to regard marriage as a prison – actually it gives you greater freedom. And you'd be amazed how many of the married men I know personally swing both ways.
>
> Some of them will even admit that they feel more at ease making love with other married men, rather than with out-and-out homosexuals, whom they're inclined to look on as somewhat wilful freaks.

Then Paddy writes to his wife. If she gets hysterical long-distance calls from a terribly disturbed young boy named Tom, she is not to be upset:

> Penny dearest, for the sake of our whole future together, I appeal to you – accept me as I am. Will you try to do that? Will you let me be silly sometimes, and show me you know it's only silliness and doesn't matter to you? Let me run off now and

70

then, looking for my teenage self and flexing my muscles! I can promise you one thing, I shall always return from these idiotic adventures with increased love for you, and gratitude – in fact, I can only enjoy the adventures if you'll sanction them!

These martyrs and chauvinists exist in real life. Many of the homosexual men interviewed for this book stressed how sexually satisfied their wives were (which cannot be denied – who is to say what happens between husband and wife?) but also how stoically the women had borne the occasional venereal disease that came their way. It seems discourteous for an author to use against him the words of a busy man who took the time to come for an interview to speak frankly about his marriage, but here is what he said:

'We're a close family, with no problems. My son is married and lives near here. He will be coming to us for Christmas. We've brought them up well, especially my wife. I'm not sure when I started cruising. I gradually found other men exciting. My wife knows but she is a remarkable woman, a very non-curious woman. It is perhaps surprising that she's never asked me where I've been, but she's a very private person. Her attitude has made it easy for me. I have the best of both worlds. I play the game by certain rules. I'm a journalist and spend a certain amount of time at conferences out of town. Most of my active gay life is in other cities.

'This may surprise you. I am faithful to my wife. I sleep with my wife. There are just some things I need that she can't supply. What? Even a slightly unshaven chin I find erotic. I tend to be very promiscuous and not having lasting relationships. She accepts it and lives with it because she loves me. I have had every sort of venereal disease. And have passed them all on to my wife. She's never complained. It's a measure of the sort of woman she is. She's had treatment; we've been to the same VD clinic.

'Saintly? I don't know. She's a schoolteacher and brings home an awful lot of exercise books to correct. A lot of her energy goes into the school and local youth clubs. We never talk about divorce. I've no regrets. I'm very conscious of how fortunate I am. I'm very happy at home and with our relationship.'

Men who know they are gay and marry without telling are playing a dirty trick. What is also common, however, is the man who tells the woman before the marriage only to have her brush the information aside. Norman and Rosemary say they have an open marriage. They are not bound by the patterns of the past. He is handsome, gaunt, pale, silent; she is animated, with high colouring. By mutual consent, she is expecting their first baby. She gives him a night out a week, and he gives her a night out. Once you've decided to break with the conventional mould, you've got to make your own rules, they agree. When Norman leaves for his free night, Rosemary says, 'See you in the morning,' just to protect herself. The first time she waited up all night and he didn't come home. Now she expects it. Sometimes he's back at midnight. Then she teases him and says, 'What are you doing here?'

If he stays out all night, she assumes he's had sex. She has slept with other men too – to show that she could do it really, to show that the option was available to her. When he first told her he was gay, they went to bed for about a week. It was the most fantastic bliss. How will their deal work when she has to get up on these nights alone, to sit with a crying baby that won't go back to sleep? They'll work that out when they come to it.

To any outsider, most women married to gay men seem to have made a bad bargain, providing yet another example of the woman being used, without protest. A psychiatrist who specializes in family interactions, hearing a gay-straight couple describe their arrangement, refused to agree that the pact was mutually beneficial. The sexual climax is import-ant in holding a marriage together, he said, because it releases the tensions between husband and wife. If you have a marriage where there is no sexual intercourse, and no prospect of it, where does the tension go? It is bound to affect the children. The father's homosexuality, he insisted,

72

is a problem for the family, not just a wife's problem. He told the wife, 'If he's comfortable and you're miserable, you're colluding with him. You're paying him back with your pain and depression. Your infant daughter will feel that. She'll grow up feeling, "I know Mummy needs me because Daddy needs Frank." In a marriage, the suffering must be shared equally, and the happiness. As a psychiatrist, he could not see what difference it made that her husband had gone off with a man rather than a woman, but, he said, 'I can't accept the word "gay". It is part of the ideological warfare. The straight partner is made to feel the miserable one. I don't think the wife should accept the connotation of the word "gay"', he said. 'And when you consider the frenetic promiscuity of many male homosexuals, calling it "gay" is a way of denying that it is also sad.'

A harsh verdict, which must make room for the fact that many of these women are married to men they love. A Unitarian gay minister in Boston, the Rev. Robert Wheatly, does worry about these wives who settle for too little. At the same time there are women whose acceptance is genuine, not masochistic, and who expand conventional ideas of how people can be together. As for the others: 'We all make constant compromises. All the time we settle for less than we want because we need to get on with life. You can't tell a person who's made that particular compromise – allowing the other partner his or her homosexuality – that to you, it looks like a sacrifice.'

6

What Every Woman Should Know

If choosing a homosexual for a husband usually takes a rare kind of innocence, it occasionally requires instead a world-weary brand of experience. The older woman with a young gay husband in tow is a stock character, and who is to say that – like Jack Sprat and his wife – they do not suit each other very well? The bargain is explicit – her money for his looks, her motherly protection for his male presence. Gloria Steinem in *New York Magazine* has suggested that this well-known combination has moved further down the age-scale. In Manhattan there are now frequently to be seen, she writes, the New Couple and the New Marriage – the beautiful, intelligent, high-salaried, liberated woman, often an executive, and the handsome, tasteful, successful homosexual, who need each other as social props for that elaborate richly encrusted lifestyle that all admire, but don't have the time to lead.

Their mutual passion for Gucci shoes and matched Yorkshire terriers, according to Steinem, may be stronger than sex, and they even have a little of that occasionally, displaying in the meanwhile their love in public as they stroll with little fingers linked:

> Could they ever be so acceptable everywhere, so envied, so secure if they weren't married? Of course not. He had tried it that way but found homosexual society so . . . so limited. And a little demeaning. She found that 'mono-sexual men' (as she called them) objected to black tie parties every week, her job or her frequent suggestions that they divorce their wives and marry her.

But very few marriages can exist on social life, even in Mayfair or Beverly Hills. Chances are that the at-home dialogue of the New Marriage is no brighter than that of the old marriage of separate bedrooms or of the woman married

74

to the man young enough to be her son; it always threatens to break through the surface to dangerous waters below. Dorothy Parker, who had had dozens of lovers, found the happiest of her three marriages was to a man widely assumed to be homosexual. Alan Campbell, many years younger, was a not very successful actor who, in collaboration with his famous wife, managed to become a passably successful screenwriter. For three happy months when she was forty-two Dorothy Parker thought they might even become parents; then she miscarried. Utterly dependent on Campbell, she remarried him after divorcing him, and went into deep depression when he died in 1963 (but not before shocking a local gossip who asked what she could do to help: 'Get me a new husband,' Dorothy told her).

But she lost few chances to taunt him about his supposed effeminacy: the homosexual man who marries a sharp-tongued woman should take care. 'Did you ever see him on the stage?' she asked a friend, in Campbell's hearing. 'Well, it was like watching a performance that Vassar girls would do, all dressed as men, and you'd expect their hair to fall down any minute.' Gay or not, he went away to war and she was furious when he did not return home from London as soon as possible in 1945. Dorothy told friends that a homosexual affair was the reason. 'As for his much-vaunted war record,' she added, 'he was over there playing hostess.'

One reason why these eyes-open marriages seem tenable at the start is that many wives convince themselves and their men that they will not be jealous of their infidelities. The wife's best tactic, if she can muster it, is to extend her maternal compassion to her husband's circle. Elsa Lanchester, Charles Laughton's lifelong and devoted wife, said of his many lovers: 'I became quite good friends with some of them. It was quite nice, really.' Katharine Cornell used professional absorption: her husband and director, Guthrie McClintic, would often slip out for quick homosexual encounters while she was moving audiences to tears, but was always back in time for the third-act curtain. Less self-sufficient women cannot take the strain after a while and turn to drink, or divorce.

A musician, about thirty, whose wife is a good retail businesswoman, says that when he is touring with his band he talks to his wife every night on the telephone. 'Like she'll say, "Having a good time?" and I say, "Yes, so far" or "Not very" and she'll know what I mean. I don't tell her every single person I pick up.' This wife is one of the new breed in that she knew he was gay when they married and shrugged it off; she did not ask him for a guarantee that he wouldn't have sex with men. Trouble does come, however, when he 'gets involved'. 'Then we've had, Marilyn and me, big discussions, lots of coffee, late into the night. I suppose in every relationship there are lots of times when you have to talk things over, the whole thing, going back five years and where you are now, to see if you've still got a stable thing going.'

Two things will keep this couple going. One is that they have decided to have another baby. 'Marilyn thinks that I need a family relationship with the wife and the kid, almost as much as I need a man, because of my childhood' (dead father, rejecting mother). The other is that Marilyn has discovered that she likes sleeping with women. 'If she does turn lesbian, it would balance things out and release some of the guilt. I would be happy if she pursued it. She's had affairs with men, but only gets a kick out of the power thing. She has a thing against the ordinary, aggressive, hetero-sexual, macho, Volvo-driving male.'

Marriage apart, the sexual fascination that gay men hold for many straight women is understandable. His elusiveness particularly excites the *femme fatale*. He brings out the predator in her. 'If I can snare him' (thinks she who has conquered so many) 'then I really must be tremendous.' The more indifferent he is, the harder she tries. As a ploy (Tony Curtis used it on Marilyn Monroe in *Some Like It Hot*) it is infallible, except that the genuine gay man is not using it as a ploy. He really is indifferent, but at the same time, he probably does have a good eye for the failings in the way she dresses, in her make-up and her accent. As Henry Higgins promises Eliza Doolittle, he could make something out of her, damn it, if she will only try. Nothing is more seductive to a woman than the prospect of self-improvement. She tries; she tries harder. She probably can succeed, for a night, in getting him into bed. Then he sulkily reverts to type. Why can't a woman be more like a man? He is accustomed to her face, but no more. If she is lucky, the experience will leave her slimmer, smarter, wittier and wiser. (One woman decided that the object of her love was spurning her because she was not well-enough informed. She read the *New York Times*, daily and thoroughly, to try to rekindle the fires. She did not, but she at least had learned what deregulation was, and détente.) If she is unlucky, or unrealistic, she will wind up with a hell of a broken heart.

Yet falling in love with a homosexual can happen to any girl looking for a protector in an unfamiliar situation. It probably happens in every university every day, another form of the sexual exploitation that women students today complain about. Sometimes women students are actually seduced by their gay academic mentors; at other times they are simply undressed and left humiliated. Sometimes they themselves scheme to get reluctant advisers into bed. One American student described the shaking hands with which her bachelor professor pulled out the bed. Exploring her body in the dark, in a scholarly way, he told her, 'You have a Rubenesque figure.' Which one was Rubens? she wondered. Painter of the fat ones? She put it out of her mind to pay attention to what was happening to her lower regions: a terror-struck darting in and out. The act was over so quickly that she says she felt he was saying to himself, 'Done it! At last! And never again!' He was up first in the morning to cook breakfast. 'I'm late to class,' he said without looking at her. 'Tell them I hate them,' she said, kissing the back of his neck hoping to get him back to bed. He quickly and silently ate his share of the perfectly cooked eggs at the perfectly set table, and left. A year later, he took her out for a drink and asked her to marry him – a civilized life, bed occasionally and Europe once a year? 'No thanks,' she said.

Avoiding gay men has emerged as a problem in women's

magazines. 'If you loved a homosexual,' asked one head-line, 'could you change him? Could you live with second best? Or would it break your heart?' As a warning, Robin Katz, an American Jewish girl in London, wrote wryly in *Honey* how she had fallen in love with one Anthony: 'It was more fun to feel fully assimilated into London life by being with an Englishman.'

> 'You're too self-sufficient,' he would say. 'Of course you feel like a misfit compared with English girls. Try being more graceful, and be more of a woman.'
>
> He didn't really mean woman. If I was a woman I would have seduced him. He meant *lady*. Lady is a man-made word that many gay men use instead of female. It implies some kind of one-dimensional creature with the glamour of the 1930s film star. She's 'adored' provided she says little and doesn't have periods . . .
>
> I almost passed as a l-a-d-y. Linking my arm in Anthony's we would descend the entrance staircase at the bisexual mecca, The Sombrero. We looked like two extras from *The Great Gatsby*. I had made the transformation from an inconspicuous loser into a much more glamorous one. And now I had a new name: I was a fag hag.

Fag hags, says Katz, are the girls whose *only* friends are gay men. It is a habit as perilous as stepping into quicksand for straight girls who need non-sexual morale-boosting and it catches them at a time when they are emotionally vulnerable: 'For me, it was being lost and lonely in a new city,' she wrote. The syndrome is familiar: the girl becomes dependent on her gay friend and then idealizes him, thinking he is perfect, except for this one flaw which she can cure. She withdraws from her heterosexual friends and then sets out to usurp his gay ones. The end is inevitable, except that sometimes she lures him with a child or marriage or both first.

The woman who acts as decoy or watches her gay friend cast his eye around in a bar or dance floor or beach (what happened to Elizabeth Taylor in Tennessee Williams' *Suddenly Last Summer*) is in on a conspiracy. The gay man fears castration: she fears penetration. Together they are a perfect couple, her excitement, like his, comes from the chase – of *his* quarry.

Garbo, Callas, Garland – the list of fag hags is glittering. Surrounded by gay men, they either fell in love or took refuge with them. Callas wept over Visconti; he encouraged her as an actress as well as a singer. She wanted more but he refused. Garbo, wiser, was unmoved by Cecil Beaton's proposal. Homosexual all his life, still he had fallen in love with her. 'But you wouldn't like to see me in the morning wearing old men's pyjamas,' she said to discourage him. 'But I'd be wearing old men's pyjamas too,' he replied. She would not relent.

What do homosexuals see in these superwomen? Judy Garland was their all-time favourite; Mae West was another, so now is Bette Midler, who owes her career to a beginning in the gay baths. Mother Earth, she's seen it all, done it all, is vulnerable to the pain of love, but not (to her gay fans) breakable. 'There's no such thing as Bad Sex,' she tells her audience sagely, 'just people who don't fit together.'

Yet fag hag is a cruel expression for a relationship in which many women who had been single for much of their adult lives have found fun and comfort. To them the gay man is safe; the Duke of Windsor even tolerated one for the Duchess. The gay man provides an escort service free of charge (and sometimes pays for the tickets). Yet those film stars and millionairesses who attend glamorous functions in the company of their hairdressers or dress designers are not just hiring their body servants to fill an empty place. They are enjoying the company of confidants, reinforcers of their own femininity and razor-sharp observers of the manners and mascara of those around them. Many a woman is grateful for her gay friends. They are funny, understanding, their advice so sensible – they are men, after all. (Their gay view of a heterosexual boyfriend who may be breaking her heart can make them laugh. 'What a dreary medical man! Does he always wear white socks? Oh well, I suppose there is no accounting for tastes.')

A woman can make herself den mother to a whole nest of

gay cubs. The telephone will always ring. There is always a companion for the cinema, for the dinners when she tries a new recipe, for the special occasions when they are even more eager to dress up than she is. She laughs at their camp squabbles with each other and dries their tears. If she lands a straight husband, her gay buddies will flock to the wedding, and even, if need be, give the bride away. It's not a bad deal in sexual politics – women and gay men as allies against the macho world – as long as the woman resists the temptation to say, 'If you'd only let *me* have a chance, you'd find you're not homosexual.' The curing power of passion, unfortunately, is something everybody believes in.

Tennessee Williams, whose work is full of fag hags, has turned a short story called 'Two on a Party' into a kind of morality play for straight women and gay men. Cora, a prostitute, and Billy, an effeminate homosexual, are travelling companions as they hunt for pickups through the sleazy hotels and bars of Florida. She was too kind, Billy thought, and they are both equally worried about growing old and ugly. One night in the shared compartment of a Pullman they have sex together. It is not a great success and afterwards each tries too hard to flatter the other:

> Gee, honey, said Cora, you're a wonderful lay, you've got wonderful skin, smooth as a baby's, gee, it sure was wonderful, honey, I enjoyed it so much, I wish you had. But I know you didn't like it and it was selfish of me to start it with you.
>
> You didn't like it, he said.
>
> I swear I *loved* it, she said, but I knew that *you* didn't like it, so we won't do it again.
>
> He told Cora that she was a wonderful lay and that he had loved it every bit as much as she did and maybe more, but he agreed they'd better not do it again. Friends can't be lovers, he said.
>
> No, they can't, she agreed with a note of sadness.

Tell these cautionary tales to a single woman intent on marrying a homosexual and she will probably shrug them off, like any other warned bride. Hope will triumph over inexperience and the devil she knows – loneliness – over the devil she does not know – the urgency of male sexual needs. Even if she tries to imagine realistically her reaction to his continuing homosexual life, she cannot; their relationship so far has thrived precisely because the sexual element has been bleached out.

A New Yorker who is in her mid-forties, has never been married and has an executive job with an advertising agency has asked herself what life would be like if she married her gay friend, Hal. She has seen other women make such marriages work: 'Hal and I have been best friends for ten years. We've spent weekends together in his apartment, and we've taken trips together. We've even shared the same room. We hold hands and kiss (he's a 'toucher' and so am I) but we've never had sex. He is more fun to be with than any person I've ever known. He sends me flowers and candy and expensive presents. I would drop everything to go wherever and whenever he suggests. But marriage . . . I don't know. He lives alone, but most of his male friends are gay. He makes good money at his job with a major network, but I know he's lonely – although he puts up a good front. He gets upset if I happen to be busy – even when he calls at the last minute as he usually does. He's in his late forties now, and I expect he'll get lonelier. Perhaps I will, too. So far I like living alone and having my own way. But we see each other constantly, and the subject could very well come up. He always wants me to be with him at company parties and dinners – so much of his life is in the totally 'straight' world populated by wives.

'But if I ever seriously considered marrying him, I'd insist that we both lay down some ground rules. We'd both have to be frank about what we would expect from the other. I'm afraid I wouldn't want our life together shared with gays *en masse* – although I like most of his gay friends. I would also be a bit afraid that marriage to Hal would make me more possessive of him – and that, I know, could ruin a marriage. In those ground rules, we'd have to spell out in detail both our roles and each partner promise to play his faithfully. That's the only way marriage to Hal could work for me. But if we did make it work, life would sure be full of fun!'

7

In Public Places

> Homosexuals have no history. Their past consists of reactions to
> them.   Gay Liberation Service

The belief that homosexuality threatens the foundations of
society is as alive today as ever. The justification is not that
homosexuality deprives the state of citizens or soldiers –
overpopulation is too clear and unpopular a danger – but
that it nourishes an antisocial subculture extending even to
espionage. Homosexuals make good spies, so goes the
assumption, because they are good dissemblers. To be sure,
if statistics could be garnered from the secret files of the
world's major powers, a doctoral thesis could undoubtedly
be written showing that homosexual men form no larger
share of the ranks of double agents than they do of the
population at large. Failing such evidence, however, the
vague accusation of subversiveness will remain, supported,
by the lateral drift of fantasy, to the homosexual's lack of
children.

When the British art historian, Anthony Blunt, was
revealed in 1979 to have been a traitor and a spy for the
Russians, the main shock was the fact that his treachery
had been known in high places – indeed he had confessed it
long before he was promoted to the post of Keeper of the
Queen's Pictures. Gentlemen protect each other, it seemed.
Yet press comment in Britain and abroad feasted on Blunt's
homosexuality as well. He had been a friend of Burgess and
Maclean, Soviet agents within British Intelligence who
managed to escape to Russia in 1951 just when their own
treachery had been found out. They were also homosexuals.
The outcry soon broadened to take in others of Blunt's
generation who like him had been at Cambridge University
and had been members of the Apostles, a secret and élite
intellectual society with a strong homosexual tradition.
Why, the question formed in the public mind, did so many

of the beneficiaries of the highest expression of British culture want to betray it? The ensuing debate cast shadows on the reputations of E. M. Forster, the novelist, who had never hidden his homosexuality, and also on that of the great economist, John Maynard Keynes as well. Keynes's homosexuality, fairly well known now, was never mentioned during his long public career which stretched from World War I until his death in 1946 after he became the architect of the postwar international banking system.

It so happened the Blunt case came at a time of economic recession, when Milton Friedman's monetarism was driving out Keynesianism which holds that governments should spend their way out of recession and should borrow money to create jobs. Suddenly in late 1979, not only Keynes's theories were being offered up as the cause of inflation, but his homosexuality as well.

In its starkest form the post-Blunt barrage against Keynes appeared as part of an attack on 'homosexual imperialism'. In an article entitled 'The Manhood of the Nation' in the *Daily Telegraph*, Colin Welch charged that homosexuals are irresponsible because, for them, there is no tomorrow. The 'momentariness' of the homosexual, Welch argued, estranges or alienates him from the family and from the society of which that family is a microcosm: 'Both family and society exist in time, in the past and in the future; he only in the present.' Then Welch lit upon Keynes:

> It was Lord Keynes who said that in the long run we are all dead – a remark which would not readily occur to anyone who had or ever expected to have any children . . . It is also Lord Keynes who is widely regarded as the begetter of inflation. His views about the value of money, as about some other things, were typically short-term, momentary. He had none of the prudent father's anguished concern to pass on to his children, in undebased currency, whatever he had managed painfully to scrape together. With Lord Keynes, the homosexual enters modern public life at the highest and most influential level.

As an arch-conservative paper, the *Telegraph* might well be expected to equate the rise of homosexual freedom with the decline of the west. Yet the more dispassionate *Times* itself also asked in an editorial what price the country had paid for the Cambridge Apostles and their cult of personal relations as a substitute for a moral code. Unforgivingly, *The Times* recalled E. M. Forster's famous remark: 'If I had to choose between betraying my country and betraying my friends, I hope I should have the guts to betray my country.' Such values, *The Times* said, tended to the destruction of 'those absolute standards of loyalty on which a democratic society depends'. Then *The Times* too trained its guns not on Blunt, but on Keynes:

> It is [also] true that theirs was largely a homosexual culture, with necessary dependence on ties of friendship rather than on the functional ties of family, and a defiance of conventional sexual morality, leading to a broader moral relativism. Even in the case of Maynard Keynes, perhaps the finest product of this culture, there may be a parallel between his emotional resentment of the monetary rules which prevented inflation, and particularly the gold standard, and his need to reject the conventional sexual morality of his period. He did not like rules.

To heap ridicule upon insult, who better than Malcolm Muggeridge? Where better than in a *Time* magazine essay? Muggeridge, satiric journalist turned Christian moralist, had been at Cambridge himself in the 1920s. The Blunt affair inspired him to write the essay on 'The Eclipse of the Gentleman'. It is only common sense, he declared, that homosexuals should make gifted actors and spies but that 'their inevitable exclusion from the satisfaction of parenthood gives them a grudge against society, and therefore an instinctive sympathy with efforts to overthrow it.' Ignoring the fact that Keynes and his circle had been undergraduates at Cambridge nearly thirty years before Anthony Blunt and the left-wingers of the early 1930s, Muggeridge lumped all their betrayals together:

> I remember reading an account of Lytton Strachey sitting on a rock in the Isle of Skye, weeping over a lost lover he had shared with Maynard Keynes, and thinking to myself how perfectly they got their own back, Keynes by inventing an economic

84

theory which, after a period of spurious prosperity, must infallibly bankrupt the countries which adopt it, and Strachey by overturning the gods of the Victorian age and with them the virtues such as thrift, hard work, integrity and truthfulness which they symbolized.

The irony of this posthumous attack, more than thirty years after his death, is that Keynes was probably the most happily married homosexual of his time, certainly among his old friends in the Bloomsbury group. When the attack began, the fact of Keynes's marriage, which had shielded him from gossip during his lifetime, was totally ignored, like a cover blown, even though his widow was still alive.

'Marrying Lydia,' said Keynes's mother, Mrs Florence Keynes, who survived him, 'was the best thing Maynard ever did.' She was not referring to any shift away from homosexuality, for the Keynes family had shied away from the dreaded word.

The first full biography of Keynes, published by the economist Roy Harrod in 1951, five years after Keynes's death, respected the family's wishes. 'I hope that I have not done damage to any reputation!' wrote Harrod in his preface. And damage he could have done. Homosexual behaviour was still a crime in Britain when the biography was published and Keynes's intellectual legacy was serving the foundation of economic recovery and the welfare state. What Mrs Keynes meant was what was obvious to all who knew Keynes in his later years: his health had always been frail and his vivacious and adoring wife diverted him from his heavy cares, and pampered him and nagged him to look after himself. She may have prolonged his life by at least nine years.

In 1925, when Keynes announced his intention of marrying Lydia Lopokova, a star of the Diaghilev ballet that had captivated London around the time of World War I, his friends in the Bloomsbury group were aghast. Keynes was already on his way to dwarfing them all, apart from Virginia Woolf, as his international reputation grew. But he shared their unconventionality and their tight exclusive preoccupation with each other's complicated sexual activities.

Keynes's marriage made a breach with Bloomsbury that was never healed. He was forty-two at the time and living at 46 Gordon Square, which he had originally shared with his lover, the painter Duncan Grant. Even though Grant by this time was living with Vanessa Bell (Virginia Woolf's sister) at Charleston, a country house in Sussex, he and Vanessa used No. 46 when they came to London. Vanessa considered it hers – she had bought the lease originally, the first 'Bloomsbury' address, when her father, Sir Leslie Stephen, died in 1914 – and the house remained in the 1920s the focus for the Bloomsbury salons, parties and charades, of which Keynes was the supreme organizer.

Off stage, Lydia Lopokova was not beautiful nor even charming. She did not have drawing-room manners and boasted that she was a peasant. Her English was atrocious. But Keynes was delighted with her. Her broken English amused him – he would roar with laughter at her malapropisms. Bloomsbury knew Lydia. She was frequently seen at its parties – at one of them Keynes had danced the can-can with her. But marriage? Bloomsbury went into an orgy of malicious gossip. Roger Fry sent Clive Bell a poem about her ('I don't imagine it would please her . . .'). Lytton Strachey was scathing. Virginia Woolf predicted that Lydia would grow stout, burden Maynard with children and ruin his career. Vanessa did not want Lydia at No. 46.

Keynes did not care. He simply went and married her, on 25 August 1925, at the St Pancras registry office. Immediately they left on a train trip to Russia so that Keynes could meet Lydia's relatives as well as examine the young Soviet revolution at first hand ('Beneath the cruelty and stupidity of the New Russia some speck of the ideal may lie hid,' he wrote upon returning). However, he had put long thought into his marriage.

To women of that time, certainly within the Bloomsbury group, homosexuality was no bar to marriage. Virginia Woolf, when she was Virginia Stephen, certainly knew that Lytton Strachey was a homosexual when he proposed to her in 1909 and she had accepted. The 'engagement' lasted only a few minutes, to Strachey's intense relief. His later description of the scene in a letter to Leonard Woolf is a masterly encapsulation of the homosexual fear of women:

> The worst of it was that as the conversation went on, it became more and more obvious to me that the whole thing was impossible. The lack of understanding was so terrific! And how can a virgin be expected to understand? You see she is her name. If I were either greater or less I could have done it and could either have dominated and soared and at last made her completely mine, or I could have been contented to go without everything that makes life important . . . Her sense was absolute, and at times her supremacy was so great that I quavered . . . I was in terror lest she should kiss me.

Did Keynes need a wife to advance his career? No one has ever suggested it. On the other hand, he must have been looking for a wife, for he told Vanessa Bell at one point that he wanted to marry the painter, Barbara Bagenal (then Barbara Hiles). He never did propose , in fact, but Barbara, extremely pretty, girlish and irreverent, was one of his favourites. If he had asked her, she told the author, looking back from her late eighties, she probably would have accepted. Even though she knew that Keynes was Duncan Grant's boyfriend, she would not have been deterred because girls in those days tended to accept those who asked them and Keynes was one of her kindest and best friends. Years later, when he decided to marry Lydia, he confided his intention to Barbara, who, by then married, with sons, challenged him: 'I don't know whether you can go to bed with her,' she said. 'I'm wondering that myself,' he confessed.

Barbara Bagenal always doubted that the marriage had been consummated. 'Lydia hadn't grown enough,' she said. 'She wasn't developed. She would have been a hopeless mother. She was a charming creature, a very simple character. You see, she wasn't really civilized. Later, after Keynes had died, she was just shattered, very rocky.'

Bloomsbury's passionate preoccupation with sex was matched only by its inexperience. There was, certainly for the women, more talk than action. They liked to scandalize each other most of all, such as the day recorded in Virginia Woolf's diaries when Lytton Strachey entered a drawing-room and pointed at a stain on Vanessa Bell's white dress. 'Semen?' he asked. ('Can one really say it? I thought [wrote Virginia] and we burst out laughing.') The literati in general were a curious mixture of passion and prurience: W. B. Yeats, who dropped in occasionally, had a very delayed sexual development and did not marry until he was fifty-two. George Bernard Shaw engineered for himself a non-consummated marriage. None the less, now that Lytton Strachey's papers have been revealed, thanks to Michael Holroyd's monumental two-volume biography, it does seem clear that homosexuality was not – as Oscar Wilde had tried so hard to prove at his trials – confined to flowery words.

Of Keynes's homosexual career there seems no doubt, at least during his Cambridge period. Leonard Woolf described Keynes as 'an effete and rotten old lecher'. From his eminence as a fellow of King's, at Cambridge, he basked in the homosexual tradition of the Apostles (which were founded by Tennyson, a homosexual) and urged it upon others, such as the philosopher, Wittgenstein, as a more elegant form of love – the Higher Sodomy. He and Strachey were considered flamboyant in their homosexuality and enjoyed teasing each other about it. When Strachey was planning a trip to Italy, Keynes suggested that he push on to Tunis and provided him with a list of hotels where, at a modest rate, he could find 'bed and boy'. When Keynes was nursing a wounded ego from coming only second in the immensely difficult examination for the Civil Service (for which he had done no work) even though he had won a first-class honours degree in economics, Strachey wrote him a sardonic poem:

> 'In Memoriam J. M. K. Ob. Sept. 1906'
> Here lies the last remains of one
> Who always did what should be done.
> Who never misbehaved at table
> And loved as much as he was able.

88

Who couldn't fail to make a joke,
And, though he stammered, always spoke:
Both penetrating and polite,
A liberal and a sodomite,
An atheist and a statistician,
A man of sense without ambition.
A man of business, without bustle,
A follower of Moore and Russell.
One who, in fact, in every way,
Combined the features of the day.
By curses blest, by blessings cursed,
He didn't merely get a first.
A first he got; on that he'd reckoned;
But then he also got a second.
He got a first with modest pride;
He got a second, and he died.

There was nothing amusing about their break. When Strachey had confided in Keynes, his best friend, about how hopelessly in love he was with Duncan Grant, Keynes had accepted the confidence without revealing that he and Grant had become lovers. Strachey only learned the truth when Grant and Keynes had begun living together; his world was shattered. The worst of it was feeling such a fool, 'like a pocket handkerchief dropped on Mont Blanc'. He wept; he wrote anguished letters to Keynes, which made Keynes weep in turn, and finally went to Scotland to try to get over it, shedding the tears which nearly eighty years later would give Malcolm Muggeridge such wry amusement. It was no doubt the rejection by Duncan Grant and Keynes that led Strachey to make his bizarre proposal to Virginia Woolf.

In the end, they settled down with women, all three. Keynes and Lydia bought a farm, Tilton, in Sussex near Charleston where Duncan Grant remained with Vanessa Bell until her death in 1961 (although Grant continued to enjoy occasional homosexual encounters, mainly in London). Strachey was taken over by the boyish Dora Carrington, the ultimate fag hag, who decided in 1915 to devote her life to caring for him; a short time after he died of cancer in 1932, she killed herself.

To those who knew Keynes as a public man between the wars, there was no whiff of Edwardian inversion. The late economist and journalist, Nicholas Davenport, who worked with him for years, starting with The National Mutual Life Insurance Company, has stated that he never knew of his homosexuality. To Davenport, Keynes did not have the manners of a homosexual. Even when Keynes was living with Grant, he was writing *A Treatise on Probability*. Intense buggery, Davenport observed, was improbable during such a labour. It drained away that ever-ready erection which, in Davenport's view, drives 'good buggers like that awful Driberg'. (Tom Driberg, MP, described his two passions as left-wing politics and homosexuality. A former chairman of the Labour Party, he was a flamboyant homosexual, so far left in his sympathies that he too has been posthumously accused of being an agent of the Soviet Union. When someone disparaged the wife Driberg chose late in life, Sir Winston Churchill is said to have remarked: 'Buggers can't be choosers.')

As a husband Keynes was always amused and interested by Lydia, never embarrassed. They had an infinity of subjects to talk about. He was enormously interested in the arts: she left economics to him. The more eminent he became – they became Lord and Lady Keynes in 1942 – the more refreshed he was by her continuing caprice and lack of affectation. She accompanied him everywhere – to New York, to Washington, even to Bretton Woods, the conference in New Hampshire in 1944 which set up the International Monetary Fund and the World Bank and took the world off the gold standard. They could be seen together on wartime visits to the United States, promenading the deck in thick life jackets, a necessity on the dangerous Atlantic crossings. He would never simply dismiss her when the men and briefcases arrived, he would say that they were going to discuss business and that it might cheer her up to go to Macy's or whatever bargain basement might be convenient.

At one wartime meeting at the Keynes's suite, the arriving dignitaries were greeted by a scene of devastation.

At least a dozen bags stuffed full of bargain basement gifts for the farmers' children in Sussex had been thrown open and the contents thrown around the room. 'Lydia's lost her keys,' Keynes explained matter of factly to his high-level contingent. As the men were talking the door burst open. Lydia entered, leaping through the air. 'I have found them!' she said. 'They were in her bosom all the time,' Keynes explained to the group and the discussion continued.

Her ballet career never revived. Diaghilev's dumping her in the early 1920s may have been one reason why she accepted Keynes's proposal at the age of thirty-two. She had some minor acting roles in the Arts Theatre in Cambridge, which Keynes had started, but largely confined her dancing to spontaneous performances, in brown exercise tights, on the stair landing at Tilton.

One unexpected performance occurred on a Pullman train from New York to Washington before one wartime conference. In intense secrecy, the delegation from the British Treasury, the Board of Trade and the economic section of the Cabinet office had been shipped across the Atlantic from Glasgow and put on a train to Washington. They were not supposed to reveal that they were there. But on the way Keynes and his wife engaged in an intense discussion of ballet whereupon she arose and danced the point she was making down the train aisle full of businessmen. Any attempt to conceal that Lord and Lady Keynes were arriving had failed.

During these complicated and tense negotiations about international banking and the loan the United States would make to Britain for post war reconstruction, Keynes was working at the end of his strength. He had had numerous heart-attacks, including one in the middle of the Bretton Woods conference. Lydia protected him like a lioness, passionately reproaching him for overworking and risking his life. When asked how *she* was, she would reply, 'When Maynard is well, I am well. When he is ill, I am ill.'

When, in 1946 he suffered a mild attack during the gala reopening of Covent Garden, sponsored by the newly founded Arts Council, of which he was chairman, she

91

greeted the King and Queen on her own. A few months later when he had his final heart attack at Tilton in 1946, she was with him. She then virtually disappeared from public view and became a recluse at Tilton, inaccessible to Bloomsbury-hunters, until her death in 1981.

It is true that Keynes always, during his marriage, led two lives, spending weekdays in London in the City or at the Treasury and weekends at King's in Cambridge. One of his colleagues there maintained that Keynes had only married 'to prove that he could do the other thing'. It may have been an unconsummated marriage; ballerinas are not known for voracious sexual appetites. Keynes may have continued to seek homosexual associations; there is no evidence. But all who saw them together were convinced that it was a love match and, more, one of the happiest marriages they had ever seen.

The homosexual scandal is so open a tradition in British public life from Edward II who was put to death with a hot poker thrust in his anus in 1327 through Oscar Wilde to the present day that it is a mystery where the comparable experience has been in American public life. The answer does not lie in the British public school system nor in the rule of the nanny, although these have played their part. The evidence that gay liberation has thrown up firmly supports Kinsey: homosexuality exists in every class, in every place, in every country. ('But not in Malta,' insisted a Maltese scholar to the author.)

The more likely explanation is that with such long experience, British society has accepted the fact, although always with horror, that homosexual elements reside within it. The Oscar Wilde trials of 1895 were more explicit in their description of private parts and faecal stains on the bedsheets than any mincing detail about the use of Vaseline was during the Thorpe trial in 1979. Yet queers and fairies are antithetical to the spirit of the pioneers. With women in short supply, homosexuality on the range is a threat. To put it another way, in America, for men in public life, the marriage cover works. The evidence has been there, just ignored.

In 1964, during Lyndon Johnson's first administration filling out the term of the assassinated President Kennedy, the member of his staff closest to the President was Walter Jenkins, a quiet kindly man. According to Theodore White, Jenkins was the steady centripetal force that held things together. As the Johnson re-election campaign steamrollered towards election day in November 1964, Walter Jenkins attended a party on 7 October, to mark the opening of *Newsweek*'s new office in Washington. Shortly after leaving, he was arrested in the men's room of the central Washington YMCA and booked on charges of disorderly conduct. The Y was not a safe place for closet queens: the District of Columbia police had drilled peepholes in the walls to observe the proceedings.

A national scandal? A blow to Johnson's electoral hopes? The very opposite. The scandal was almost smothered at birth. Unlike Watergate, no enterprising reporter noticed the item on the police blotter. It took a friendly leak to the Republican National Committee from a GOP sympathizer at the FBI, who also heard it from another unofficial source. A full week later the news reached Senator Barry Goldwater, Johnson's Republican opponent, but Goldwater, a gentleman and a prude, said nothing. Even when two arch-Republican newspapers, the *Chicago Tribune* and *Cincinnati Enquirer*, learned the news, they decided against publication. It was left to the *Washington Star* to telephone the White House to check the story.

Jenkins then confessed, to Abe Fortas and Clark Gifford, Johnson's campaign masterminds, who bundled him into a hospital and personally visited Washington newspaper editors to plead for silence. However, when the news emerged that this was Jenkins's second arrest – in 1959 he had been charged, after a similar incident, with being a pervert – the story went out on the news agency wires from the city to the world. George Reedy, White House press secretary, wept openly. 'And perhaps the most amazing of all events of the campaign of 1964,' wrote White, 'is that the nation faced the fact fully – and shrugged its shoulders.'

It might be more accurate to say that the nation faced the

93

fact as fully as it had Kinsey's claim that one-third of all males had had a homosexual experience to the point of orgasm. It ignored it.

If history wants any proof that the warmth and intelligence of Lady Bird Johnson, the President's wife, were no mere press agent's fabrication, it can turn to the statement she issued at that time:

'My heart is aching today for someone who has reached the end point of exhaustion in dedicated service to his country. Walter Jenkins has been carrying incredible hours and burdens since President Kennedy's assassination. He is now receiving the medical attention which he needs. I know our family and all of his friends – and I hope all others – pray for his recovery. I know that the love of his wife and six fine children and his profound religious faith will sustain him through this period of anguish.'

As an expression of sympathy, it was superb. Mrs Johnson also helped Jenkins find a new job, with the Johnson family broadcasting station in Austin, Texas. But as a reminder to Americans that many homosexuals were husbands and fathers, that furtive sex was all that was open to most of them and that hundreds of thousands, perhaps millions of them, routinely risked arrest and disgrace, it was a failure. Walter Jenkins was written off as a medical case, the victim of an exotic malady brought on by incredible and hardly duplicable burdens. To everyone who knew the hard-driving President, the explanation was plausible.

To his lasting credit, during the campaign, Barry Goldwater refused to make capital out of the flagrant evidence of moral corruption in the White House. Not that he could have done. He was going to lose anyway. And the president? The ostentatiously coarse rancher who must have thought he could tell a queer from ten miles off? Apart from requesting Jenkins's resignation, publicly he said nothing. By election day, it was as if a stone had been dropped in a pond without making ripples or as if Walter Jenkins had slipped into a black hole in the universe. The moral was clear: a man can do funny things when he is tired.

*

Homosexuality never broke the surface of the Alger Hiss case. If it had, it might have filled in some of the missing pages on homosexuality in American public affairs. It could even be part of the answer to the question that hovers to this day: what was Whittaker Chambers's motive for hounding Alger Hiss? From 1948 until 1950, Chambers, a paunchy, paranoid ex-communist spy, accused Hiss, through endless hearings of the House Unamerican Activities Committee, FBI investigations and two trials, of having been a member of the American communist underground and having passed him stolen State Department papers. Hiss denied both having been a communist or ever knowing Chambers. In the end, Chambers succeeded, and so did Richard Nixon, the young Congressman on the committee, who used the case as a stepping stone to higher things. The elegant, polished Hiss, who in 1948 was president of the Carnegie Endowment for International Peace, who had been a high official in the State Department and who had accompanied President Roosevelt to Yalta in 1945, was convicted of perjury and sentenced to five years in prison.

The perjury charge stuck for two basic reasons: (1) State Department documents found hidden in a pumpkin on Chambers's farm in Maryland were declared after analysis to have been typed on Hiss's Woodstock typewriter; (2) Hiss so maladroitly changed his story about never having seen Chambers in his life before the day in which the House Unamerican Activities Committee, at Nixon's suggestion, brought the two of them face to face. (Perhaps he had known him, Hiss said, retracting his original denial, peering closely at Chambers's puffy face . . . if Chambers had had his very bad teeth fixed and had once gone under the name of George Crosley. Hiss turned out to have known 'Crosley' well, loaning him his house and giving him a car.)

The case and the notoriety ruined Chamber's life as well as Hiss's; it obsessed him until he died in 1961. In his autobiography, *Witness*, dedicated to 'my beloved children', he set down what he wanted them to know – that he had been subjected to a tremendous public defamation by the left-wing intellectual and liberal establishment allied with a conspiracy of Republican businessmen. He saw forces against him as moved by snobbism and guilt. His own sole motive, he claimed, was to expose the Hiss case and uncover the communist conspiracy for the nation. Since Hiss's defenders could not accept the commonsense answer as to his motives – that Hiss had been both a communist and a Soviet agent – they had to invent some. As Chambers put it:

> The old masters – Freud and the author of *Psychopathia Sexualis* – were conned again. No depravity was too bizarre to 'explain' Chambers' motives for calling Hiss a communist. No hypothesis was too preposterous, no speculation too fantastic to 'explain' how all those State Department documents came to be copied on Hiss's Woodstock typewriter. Only the truth became too preposterous to entertain.

In other words his enemies had insinuated that Chambers had been a homosexual. They were right. He had been – but they did not know it for a certainty. However, Chambers, suppressing the truth for his children and posterity, was nonetheless correct saying that the search for psychological motives was desperate among Hiss's liberal supporters who passionately believed in his innocence. They saw the case against Hiss as a Cold War attempt by Republicans to accuse the Roosevelt-Truman administrations of being soft on communism and would have liked to use the many rumours of Chambers's homosexuality to discredit him. At two trials, the Hiss defence lawyers did rely heavily on psychiatric interpretations of Chambers's unsettled personality, of his reaction to his brother's suicide, his paranoia, and pathological lying. Hiss did allow himself to refer to his accuser as 'somewhat queer' several times. The evidence, however, was not solid enough. The Hiss side had another reason for restraint. The FBI had been interviewing friends and doctors of Hiss's troubled stepson, Timothy Hobson, who had been discharged from the Navy on emotional grounds relating to homosexuality. J. Edgar Hoover, head of the bureau, passed on to an agent in New York the words of an informant who said that Hiss

96

was ready to sacrifice his stepson's reputation in order to save himself. The reverse was true. To ward off any possible counterattack against his wife's son, Hiss held back from pursuing evidence which might have swung the balance of the case.

In fact, unbeknown to the defence team, and Hiss, Chambers had confessed a lurid homosexual past to the FBI before the first trial began. Knowing that the Hiss side was scouring his life for anything which could discredit him as a witness, Chambers (two months after a suicide attempt) decided that he had better tell the government just how vulnerable he, its star witness, was. As if he could not bear to see the look on their faces when the news first struck them, Chambers handed a letter to an FBI agent in New York and left for Baltimore. It would all come out at the trial anyway, he thought. In the letter he asked for a special interview, with only one agent present, in which he would testify to things, 'which should be told only to a priest'.

The story, taken from statements made to the FBI in 1949 and revealed in Allen Weinstein's *Perjury*, a major analysis of the case published in 1978 (which found Hiss guilty), showed Chambers as one of those middle-class Depression radicals who romanticized the poor – and also as a cruising homosexual. Chambers traced the onset of this behaviour to a night in 1933 or 1934 when a young man, a miner's son, stopped him on the street and asked Chambers to give him food and lodging. Chambers agreed, and took him to an hotel.

There he . . . taught me an experience I did not know existed. At the same time, he revealed to me and unleashed, the . . . tendency of which I was still unaware. It was a revelation to me. As a matter of fact it set off a chain reaction in me which was almost impossible to control. Because it had been repressed so long, it was all the more violent when once set free.

I do not know the identity of the young man I spoke of, nor does he know my true identity. I have never seen him since the first night I met him. For three or four years, I fought a wavering battle against this affliction. Since that time (in 1933 or 1934), and continuing up to the year of 1938, I engaged in numerous homosexual activities both in New York and Washington DC. At first I was engaged in these activities whenever by accident the opportunity presented itself. However, after a while the desire became greater and I actively sought out the opportunities for homosexual relationships. I recall that incidents of this nature took place in the Hotel Annapolis and the Hotel Pennsylvania in Washington DC. I registered in these hotels under assumed names which I cannot now recall. I know that other incidents took place in hotels in New York City which I cannot now remember, but concerning which I might state that they were the typical 'flea bag' type of hotel one finds in certain parts of Manhattan. I never had any prolonged affairs with any one man and never visited any known places where these type of people were known to congregate. I generally went to parks and other parts of town where these people were likely to be found.

I am positive that no man with whom I had these relations during this period ever knew my true identity, nor do I at this time recall the names of any of them.

The experience was particularly devastating to Chambers, as it had occurred about the time his first child was born. He had married his wife, Esther, in 1931 after several affairs with women which had included an abortion and communal sex. After a miserable childhood, he had desperately wanted a normal family life. To the FBI, Chambers insisted that he had sloughed off homosexuality along with the Communist Party. For years, he said in 1949, he had been living a blameless and devoted life as husband and father:

The Hiss forces, of course, will seek to prove that my weakness entered into my relations with Alger Hiss and possibly others. This is completely untrue. At no time, did I have such relations, or even the thought of such relations with Hiss or with anybody else in the Communist Party or connected with Communist work of any kind. I kept my secret as jealously from my associates in the CP as I did from everyone else. I tell it now only because in this case, I stand for the truth. Having testified mercilessly against others, it has become my function to testify mercilessly against myself. I have said before that I am consciously destroying myself. This is not from love of self-

98

destruction but because only if we are consciously prepared to destroy ourselves in the struggle can the thing we are fighting be destroyed.

In 1975, with these revelations under the Freedom of Information Act, Alger Hiss, still seeking vindication, said publicly for the first time that he believed Chambers's motivation to have been that of a 'spurned homosexual' seeking revenge for an unrequited attraction. No evidence has suggested that the abundant rumours that Hiss himself was homosexually inclined were true.

It is all too easy today to ascribe sexual motives to inexplicable actions, just as it is virtually impossible to reconstruct the ideological preoccupations of the 1930s. 'We will never be able to nail the Hiss case down sexually,' Allen Weinstein told the author, 'and we don't need it to explain its intensity.'

What the FBI papers on Chambers do display is how the psychological technique of splitting works equally well for the closet homosexual as for the secret agent. Chambers had many lives in watertight compartments of which these were just two. Over his lifetime, he used at least eleven aliases; he spoke many languages fluently and could also produce English with a convincing foreign accent. His wife said that she did not even know he was a secret agent, let alone a homosexual. He underwent several major changes of personality, from communist to senior editor of *Time*, to arch-Christian and patriotic informer. He also was a man who went through intense inner torment and loneliness, finding in the end the justification for his suffering in his beloved children. They have repaid him with loyalty and today do not believe that their father's confession is genuine.

How long will it be before homosexuality goes the way of adultery and becomes too commonplace to ruin a political career? Since homosexuality was declassified as a mental illness in 1973 (see Chapter 11), the outlook for homosexuals in public life has improved dramatically. Since 1975 when the then Civil Service Commission in the United behaviour became known – Walt Whitman lost his job at the Department of the Interior in 1895 because of the homosexual content of his poetry – the federal government has become, as for other minorities, a haven of job security and professional advancement.

So far have federal agencies moved from automatic dismissal of homosexuals that the National Security Agency, a branch of the Defense Department, gave a gay man a top secret security clearance on the condition that he tell his parents and relatives of his homosexuality and thus eliminate the possibility that he might be vulnerable to blackmail. The Navy Vice-Admiral who made the controversial decision was later, with the unanimous approval of the Senate, made deputy director of the Central Intelligence Agency.

Correspondingly, Washington DC has attracted a large gay population. While some gays, according to the *Washington Star*, which in 1980 ran a seven-part series on the phenomenon, felt the capital was a 'closet San Francisco' because of the need in many politically sensitive jobs to keep gayness secret, other homosexuals called it a near-Utopia. For them, Washington offers along with job security, a transient urban population and style of life suited to single people, a proliferation of gay bars, restaurants, housing complexes and gay political organizations.

Government jobs are one thing; elected office another. The electorate still likes its political representatives and their aides to be straight, preferably married. At long last, however, the American public has begun to accept that Washington sex scandals no longer are, in the words of the *Washington Star*, 'as predictably heterosexual as a travelling salesman joke'.

The first homosexual scandal of 1980 saw Robert Bauman, the Maryland Republican mentioned earlier, charged with soliciting sex from a sixteen-year-old boy, and Bauman promptly resigned, promising to seek treatment. The press noted that Bauman had been an active campaigner against homosexual rights. Virtually at the same time came the more complicated case of Representative Jon Hinson from Mississippi, also a Republican. As he prepared to run for re-election in November 1980, Hinson called a press conference to volunteer two confessions: first, he had concealed from public knowledge that he had been among the six survivors of a fire in 1977 at a Washington gay film club in which eight men died. Second was that he, an ex-Marine, had been arrested in 1976 for committing an obscene act in front of the Iwo Jima Marine Memorial in Arlington, Virginia, a known rendezvous for male homosexuals. Hinson, with his wife at his side, swore that he was not homosexual and was re-elected. Three months later he was arrested in a men's room on Capitol Hill with a male employee of the Library of Congress, for 'attempted sodomy' – the kinder of the two charges open to the US Attorney's Office. 'Attempted sodomy' is a misdemeanour which carries a maximum penalty on conviction of a year in prison, a $1,000 fine or both. Sodomy itself is a felony, with a maximum penalty of ten years in prison. Hinson took himself to a locked ward of Washington's Sibley Hospital, and from there resigned.

Times had changed to the extent that a newspaper in Jackson, Mississippi, far from blushing, wanted to know which man was passive and which active in the men's room incident, while the director of the Mississippi Gay Alliance, Edward Sandifer, stated, 'We feel it is the repression of society that drove the congressman from the bedroom to the bathroom.' If there were any reason for Hinson to resign, Sandifer said, it was his failure to support gay rights.

One way to handle such crises in the future may have been indicated by the candour of a Congressman from the more tolerant district of Bedford-Stuyvesant in Brooklyn. When Representative Fred Richmond, a Democrat and millionaire, was arrested in 1978 on a homosexual morals case, he got the charge dropped by agreeing to participate in a first offender programme. Then he wrote to the people of his district asking for their compassion and understanding. That year and again in 1980, he was re-elected with a handsome majority.

Homosexuality does no harm to a reputation if the

101

statesman is dead, like Dag Hammarskjöld. In the arts, homosexuality is now perfectly respectable. Queen Elizabeth II not only gave the Order of Merit to the composer, Benjamin Britten (the OM had probably been withheld from E. M. Forster until he was eighty-nine because of his homosexuality), but sent a letter of condolence, when he died, to his longtime companion, Sir Peter Pears. Even in Britain, however, where adult homosexual acts have been legal since 1967, there are, at the time of writing, no self-acknowledged homosexuals in the public eye, outside the arts. Entertainers and television personalities are very reluctant to 'come out'.

In Allen Drury's *Advise and Consent*, a *roman à clef* of Washington written in 1960, the fictional Senator Anderson shot himself when his homosexuality was exposed. Now, even a senator would be unlikely to commit suicide in such an event. Yet he would hardly expect re-election. For a woman, to be female is in itself such a bar to getting into the Senate, that the theoretical added handicap of lesbianism is not worth considering.

As long as homosexuality can still be equated with treachery, as long as there are so many laws making the homosexual as criminal as the bank robber, and as long as public opinion so strongly disapproves, the homosexual will have a difficult time trying to build a political career, even as a single person.

8

Lesbians and Wives

'It is still true that most women are married, or have been, or plan to be, or suffer from not being.'

Simone de Beauvoir, *The Second Sex*

There are three main differences between male and female homosexuals who marry: women do not face the same either-or choice between marriage and parenthood; women, lesbian or straight, are more interested than male gays in settling down with one person and forming a couple; most lesbians who have been married say they did not realize their homosexuality until after they had married.

Surely, the women's movement may say, lesbian women do not stay with their husbands if they were foolish enough to marry in the first place? The voice of lesbian feminism has declared so loudly, so often, 'Be gay, be gay, to collude with men is to be a traitor', that a woman like Kate Millett who wants to be a lesbian in the movement must shed her husband. Radical feminists find it difficult even to be bisexual. Debbie Lewis, writing about her bisexuality in *Women: A Journal of Liberation*, confessed, 'I feel particularly cowardly because at the present time I'm in a relationship with a man and not with a woman (though open to that possibility). In some ways, coming out as a bisexual has been harder for me than my original coming out into the supportive lesbian community . . .'

No doubt many lesbians who married before women's liberation took hold (about six years before gay liberation, dating the birth of the women's movement from the publication of *The Feminine Mystique* in 1963 and gay liberation from the Stonewall riots in Greenwich Village in 1969) would agree with the lesbian, now in her late thirties, who says, 'If I had been born five years later, I never would have married. I might still have had a child though. In spite of all the garbage that goes on, I've enjoyed motherhood. It

103

would have been easier, in fact, if I didn't have to deal with a father.'

Yet many homosexual women marry, and many stay married. Many do not tell their husbands. The Kinsey San Francisco study documented the fact that homosexual women were more likely to have married than were homosexual men, and those who did enjoyed it less. More than a third of the white and nearly half of the black women in its large sample had been married at least once. Compared with their straight sisters, the lesbians tended to be younger when they got married – the average age was twenty-one and nearly half had been brides before nineteen. Once married, they had intercourse a lot less often, and by the time the marriage broke up – as most did within the first three years – about a quarter were having no sex at all with their husbands.

Half of the white women did not consider themselves lesbians when they married. Nearly half of those who suspected it did not tell their husbands. More of the black women knew about their orientation but fewer passed on the information.

The findings add up to a picture of the enormous social pressure there still is upon women to get married. They also show how much later than men women awaken sexually. Male gays may marry to convince themselves they are straight. The women tend to think they *are* straight; have they not been dating like the rest? Their mothers, families and friends expect them to marry and they do. It is often only when they have had a taste of sexual intercourse, with or without an enlightening homosexual experience, that it dawns on them where they must seek their pleasure. One young woman from Brooklyn confesses that the night she realized she was really lesbian, she wrote in her diary, 'Thank God, I never have to get fucked again!'

Her decision, taken at the age of twenty-seven, does make one wonder what a lesbian is. According to her, she had had an accountant for a husband who would not let her talk during intercourse (and she is a talker) because it spoiled his concentration. Was she lesbian, or just unlucky? Even clinical psychologists recognize these days the 'political lesbian' who has made the switch to females on purely ideological grounds. This woman convert insists that she is a lesbian in spite of the fact that she has not yet had a sexual experience with a woman. Plenty of women have offered to bring her out, she says, but she has refused. She wants the first time to be overwhelming, to be so passionate that she cannot stop herself. When, on the several occasions she has found herself ready to take the plunge, the other woman she chose was committed to someone else. Not yet even divorced, but separated for nearly a year, she now lives in a lesbian society and is taking instruction, as a convert might do for baptism.

'Just because I'm a lesbian doesn't mean I can't have sex with men. I like men. That's just not the way I want to be. I think we are all trying to fit into little compartments. It takes a while to realize that that is not how life is. Becoming lesbian, I've learned that some things are Politically Correct and others are Politically Incorrect. Natural fibres are correct; synthetics are politically incorrect. Diaphragms are correct; the pill is incorrect. Children are correct – if you put them in day care. Marriage, of course, is incorrect. Bras and shaving your legs are politically incorrect. Shaving under your arms is incorrect too, but it gets very hot in New York in the summer. Okay, I'm a dyke, but if I smell under my arms, I'll shave under my arms.'

The experience and problems of lesbian mothers will be discussed in Chapter 10. The fact is that many homosexual women who felt that marriage was the only way to have children in the past are still living within those marriages. Like their male counterpart, they have to face the question – to tell or not to tell? For mothers it is the choice between living a double life or risking losing the children in a custody fight.

Come out? This fortyish mother of three sons cannot think of anything less likely. She is active in the PTA, the church council and her local branch of the Women's Institute. Her husband is a lawyer for an insurance company. A size 16, confident, pleasant-looking woman with swinging hair and a duffle coat, there are a dozen of her waiting in estate cars outside any surburban primary school in the afternoon.

Since she was twenty she knew she was excited by women. She found out from a married woman, a friend of the family. They had been spending a lot of time together, and one afternoon, they found themselves in bed. It was the most wonderful thing that had ever happened to her. Then the friend's husband died. Even though he had cancer, both women were stricken with guilt, as if they had killed him. They never made love again and although that was over twenty years ago and they are still friends, they never refer to it.

After that, she had a lot of boyfriends. A few years later, on her birthday, she thought, 'I've got to find out what it's all about', and when the young man who had invited her out missed the last bus, she invited him to stay at her place. She liked his looks. She put him in the spare room but then went in and said 'Charles, this is ridiculous.' She got in bed with him. What happened didn't revolt her; but it didn't do anything for her either. It told her what she had always known, that basically she must be a lesbian. 'It is something I'll outgrow,' she thought. 'If I don't outgrow it, I'll submerge it. I'll get married.' She wanted children.

Fate did not hurry, but eventually sent the ideal man along – from the same background, established in his firm, more than a dozen years older. In a gentlemanly way, he proposed. They did not go to bed until she had accepted, but when they did it was wonderful. That was all it needed, she told herself at the time – the thought of wedding bells. She should have known that a man doesn't reach middle life without getting married without a reason. As she learned later, he had never been to bed with anyone before who wasn't a prostitute.

Even before the marriage, the sex trailed off. She was worried, being so anxious to have children – but there were always reasons why they couldn't make love. Like a fool, she ignored the warning signs.

106

For four years no children appeared. As her thirties advanced she began to panic, and consulted infertility clinics. The gynaecologists would ask: 'How often do you make love?' and when she said, 'Hardly ever,' they would laugh. What did she expect?

Then jackpot. Two acts of intercourse in two years produced two sons, and another boy appeared two years later, the results of single dogged encounters. She was an expert by this time at the whole procreation business – taking the temperature to get the fertility time right, natural childbirth exercises and breast-feeding. She has loved every minute of it, except the male intervention. The boys are exceptional, bright and funny. If she were fifteen years younger, she thinks she would have had the kids without being married. Her marriage is miserable. Her marriage is nothing.

In spite of, or because of, her pleasure in motherhood, she felt confident enough to explore her lesbianism again. Inspired by a friend, she went to a bar where lesbians gather, and carefully drank tonic water with no gin. What is uglier than a drunk woman? She got into conversation with an attractive woman and found herself making a date for Saturday night. They met, wasted little time over dinner and went back to the woman's flat and made love. 'It was fantastic. I felt as if I was being dragged back into reality. I was being shown the truth. I really flipped. I went really overboard. I think I frightened her to death. It changed my life. Not hers. She was a practising lesbian. To her I was just another lay.'

Where does that leave this pillar of the community, mother of three? Married. She feels she cannot possibly take a job with her children so young, nor can she leave town. Her whole identity, apart from this newly discovered dimension, is there. What her husband does for sex, she does not know and does not ask. Between them, husband and wife have a balance of secrecy. He is a good, if distant, father to the boys. He puts them to bed if she is out and reads to them. He is basically a good man, impersonal, but kind. Not even a male chauvinist pig. He is nice. There is no

107

way she can duck out of that. One thing she has discovered: some women's clothes, silky lingerie mostly, in a box in the cellar. He knows, she says, that she has found them. She has said nothing, hoarding the information for ammunition in case she ever needs to defend herself, in a custody case, perhaps. She has not looked recently to see if the box is still there.

Among lesbians, a gulf exists between those who have been married and those who have not, and also between those who have had children and those who have not. It often boils down, says one woman, to the difference between 'nouveau lesbians' and 'lifelong lesbians'. How *could* you sleep with a man? the first asks the second. If the late-blossomer answers, 'It wasn't so bad' or 'I really enjoyed it,' she may stir up anger or envy or resentment. A lesbian who has resolutely kept the faith and suffered the isolation of homosexuality all her adult life may feel that the late lesbian sold out early and has had the best of both worlds. And may sell out again. Or, the diehard lesbian may not like the trappings of family life cluttering up her home. One lesbian mother says, 'Sharing life with my twelve-year-old Chris was difficult for my friend Jane at first. He talks like a twelve-year-old. He has lots of energy and a lot to say.'

None the less, the older woman who becomes lesbian after a long stretch of marriage is increasingly common. For some, like the PTA mother just described, it is a case of long-suppressed homosexuality emerging at last. For others, it is a flight from depression and a return in fantasy to her own mother or it may consolidate her feminine identity at a time in her life when that is threatened – by children leaving home, by her husband's losing interest or the deterioration of her own attractiveness. Very often these homosexual relationships in middle-age are not visible, unless the women choose to proclaim them.

The western world has always been more tolerant of lesbians than of male homosexuals, for several reasons. First, it simply has not needed to notice them. The asexual spinster is a believable and familiar figure and, single or

108

married, lesbian women have much more in common with heterosexual women than gay men do with their straight counterparts – as the women's movement has demonstrated. Second, lesbianism has not been seen to undermine the economic position of the family. A male homosexual was thought to abdicate the male duty to support a wife and children. Third, it has been customary for most adult women to have psychologically intimate friendships with other women; a psychoanalytic interpretation of these friendships is that they represent the infant's close tie with the mother – an approximation which adult heterosexual males can find in their wives. Fourth, lesbian lovemaking is seen as less unnatural and less disgusting. Anal intercourse, because of its association with defecation, has been particularly abhorred. (As an Irishman, delicately referring to the practice, said to the author: 'An unnatural orifice, surely you'll agree?') A feminist explanation of the abhorrence of buggery must be that it is the reverse of phallus worship: the penis is too important to be put in the wrong place. As women do not possess such a valuable part, it does not matter what they do with what they have instead.

Few western countries have instigated laws against female homosexuality. It is commonly believed that when the 1885 Criminal Law Amendment Act, which declared all male homosexual acts in private as well as in public to be illegal, was going through Parliament, the wording was restricted to males because Queen Victoria, who had to approve all legislation, could not understand how two women could perform a sexual act together and no one cared to explain it to her.

Myra would have done. She is a teacher, married with one daughter and one son, exuberantly Jewish and newly lesbian. In a roomful of lesbians she stands out as a sexy woman, not by her clothes – the blue jeans and man's shirt are uniform – but by her well-cut, streaked blonde hair and film-star smile. She has told her husband about her change and she has no intention whatsoever of getting divorced. With plenty of basis for comparison, she can articulate the difference between the two ways of making love:

109

'I'm celebrating my twenty-second wedding anniversary tomorrow. I'm just a conventional little North London Jewish girl who married a North London Jewish boy. We've got a girl and a boy. It was after I had them, when I was thirty-one or thirty-two, that I began training as a teacher.

'When I met Lesley, when I first started teaching, she was really just a good close friend that I could share everything with. She's had a lot of pain. She's thirty-four; never been married. We wrote letters to each other if we were apart. There was never anything physical, or sex. If she was crying, I would hold her. We went on trips together. A few months ago, we went on holiday to Corfu – she with her mother, me with my husband. Her mother is overbearing. My husband's a sweetie. I love him dearly. Lesley and I had an awful fight at the end of the holiday. She accused me of having mixed values. I was terribly upset. I realized she'd meant more to me than I knew. About the same time, I read *The Women's Room*. It changed my life. It showed me how women were always second best to men.

'My husband and I had a good strong sex life, but he's not good in bed. I found lots of other men who were. I had never told him because he didn't want to hear, but when I began to think of the traps that women get into, how I thought that my house was the centre of my life, I told him.

'One evening I met Lesley casually. She was talking about her relationships to men, how she'd never found it easy to climax.

'"I think I'm into women," she said. "So am I," I said, meaning Women's Lib. Then she said, "I've fallen in love with Jackie," another teacher. "She has been gay, but now she's straight." I wept and said, "How could you!" I was in turmoil. I couldn't believe how upset I was. I couldn't work . . . I couldn't think straight. "What *am* I?" I kept asking myself. Finally I told Lesley direct: "I just want to go to bed with you."

'She was frightened, but I said "Let's try." For a week, let me tell you, I was so turned on by the thought of what we could do together . . . I had no hangups with sex, I've always enjoyed it. I liked to feel that I was in touch with all my sexuality. Finally, she asked me over to her place. We just made love, it was fantastic. It did more for me than anything I've ever had with a man. It was so *reciprocal.* There was no power thing as there is with a man. I know that I was pleasuring her because I knew what she was feeling. I was elated, on a high; I felt wonderful.

'When I told Sid, my husband, he said, "Great! Can I watch?"

'I'm really anti-men. They don't think we're very important. What we do is trivial. Look at the jobs they hold! I think that is why they find the idea of lesbian lovemaking a turn-on. He would be very jealous if I was having an affair with a man.'

At first Myra thought of reorganizing her whole way of life. She took a cheap flat of her own and debated whether or not to set up housekeeping with Lesley. Both were very agitated: Lesley's mother, suspecting what was going on, was scathing. Myra's children didn't take it very well. The daughter said she couldn't stand Lesley; the young son simply would not mention her name at all. The daughter did admit curiosity:

' "What do you and Lesley do?" she asked me. "Do you do this and that?" I answered, "I *did* tell you what Daddy and I do in bed but I won't tell you what I do with Lesley." My husband asked too: "Do you use a dildo?"

' "No," I said. "I'm not trying to substitute a prick. If I wanted a prick, I'd go out and *get* a prick." For a while, I thought I could still be aroused by a man. At a party, recently there was one of these flashes – when you know there can be something – but finally last week I went to lunch at his studio. He was attractive, much-travelled, an Israeli, politics were right, forty-five years old, everything designed to drop you into bed. I met him and his wife through my husband. A couple of days after the party, he called me and said, "I want to get to know you better." So I went. But there was no interest. Last year I would have been tearing around, scheming about a way to go away for a weekend.

'It's a fundamental change in my sexuality. I've never

111

known such satisfaction. In the past, yearning or longing, I felt I was oversexed. I was pushed by some strong physical urge that sent me out chasing them. Now I just feel very good.

'I never stop to question whether I am a lesbian or not. Lesley questions all the time: was I born this way, was it my mother, was it because I grew up without a father?

'Whether I'm a lesbian and want all women, or whether becoming lovers was just an extension of my relationship with Lesley, I don't know. I've never had a relationship with another woman. You see, I've done everything society has expected of me – married, had kids. But Lesley's under pressure: she's thirty-four and has a real longing for kids. Artificial insemination is out; she's very fixed on knowing who a child's father is, having grown up without one. I'd love her to get pregnant; that would fulfil her, and would form her.

'Sex isn't that different an experience with women than with men. I don't have more orgasms than before. We do all the things you would do with a man – oral sex, manual manipulation, mutual masturbation, but it's not geared to orgasms like it is with a man. He comes; then he turns over and goes to sleep. With a woman, you can go on after and if an orgasm doesn't happen, it doesn't matter. The whole thing goes on much much longer – two or three hours we can spend. Last night we went to bed at nine o'clock and didn't go to sleep until one-thirty in the morning. It just doesn't have a beginning and an end, and the orgasms are even better.

'While making love to men I've always thought of women and I've always had lesbian fantasies and dreams. I've felt more feminine since I've discovered lesbianism. I don't want to look too masculine and am not interested in role-playing. It's a marvellous feeling that nothing is taboo, that there is none of my sexuality that I haven't explored. I've read a lot since I went gay and I've come out at work. The headmaster is gay; he considers himself married. "You are a very surprising lady," he said when I told him. "I never would have dreamt it." I've also told my parents.

112

My mother was really freaked out, more by the idea of my taking a place of my own. My father . . . oh, dear. That's a different scene altogether. I was the apple of his eye, his eldest daughter. I was always closer to him than to Mummy. He said to her, "How could she become so *perverted*?" My sister-in-law, who adores Sid, her brother, is very upset.

'The future? I've never been a planner. I'm happy with things as they are. I was ready to leave Sid but when I started moving odds and ends out, it was such a wrench. I still do his shirts and things like that. I'm not that liberated. I get up at half-past five or six in the morning to make all sorts of meals and shove them in the freezer. When I go away, I first sort out the laundry and do the big shopping. Economically, I'm self-sufficient. The flat is very cheap. We've got a joint account, Sid and me, and when I buy food I use his money. My salary gets paid into my account and his into our joint account. I'm meticulous with his money, but if I did leave him I would drop my living standards quite a bit.

'We still take holidays together, Sid and I. We're going on a walking trip together in Dorset next week. We both like walking. We have an easy warmth and companionship together. He avoids talking about my lesbianism. Sid says, "I love you and don't want to lose you and whatever you want to do is all right with me."'

To be a lesbian and a wife is no more a contradiction in terms now than it was in the past. For better or worse, women need men, or many of them do, and men respond. Women's economic dependence on men has lessened, but hardly vanished, although their need for a man's physical strength may have done so. Few women today, thanks to electronics and automation, need to envy with awe the man who can, as the boyish March had to watch in D. H. Lawrence's *The Fox*, cut down at a stroke the tree that she has been punily hacking away at for a week:

Then suddenly his form seemed to flash up enormously tall and fearful, he gave two swift flashing blows, in immediate succession, the tree was severed, turning slowly, spinning strangely in the air and coming down like a sudden darkness on the earth.

Lawrence's heroine was swiftly punished for turning the job over to a superior male. The tree crashed (as the man calculated) onto the neck of her female lover, killing her, and March then had to marry the axe-man and emigrate to Canada.

Women still need a protector to do some of what they want to do. The following letter was written to the author from an isolated community near the Canadian border in 1980:

'I've seen lesbianism as a valuable self-affirming facet of my personality since age thirteen. At eighteen I met my "husband". He knew of my sexual orientation before we had a private conversation. He is heterosexual. Four years have passed. We have a 1-yr-old son and are expecting the birth of our second child in late Nov. – early Dec . . . We are applying for public assistance, keeping track of the very spare local job listings and comparing schools.'

Who needs a man? She does. The affinity between today's married lesbians and those of the turn of the century may be greater than it seems, for they feel protective as well as in need of protection. They would not let their man down.

In 1901, Kate Salt, the raven-haired literary wife of George Bernard Shaw's fellow socialist and vegetarian friend Henry Salt, wrote to a homosexual friend, Edward Carpenter, of her guilt as a lesbian, at having bound her husband to an unconsummated marriage: '. . . we two poor things dwelling here together like friendly strangers – no touch possible (oh! the pity of it!) and no understanding. But 20 years brings deep chains that could never be cut through.'

Kate described how, after a week with her lover, Mary, in Yorkshire, when Henry had joined them, and Mary had gone to another house to sleep, a remorseful love for her husband swept over her: 'I had never before realized *what* I had done in letting myself get married. At the same time, such profound *Pity* took hold of me, seeing as for the first

114

time what I had done to *him* by marrying him, that I believe he was safe from that moment – I mean I could never have thought again of deserting him – poor lonely thing.'

When it works, such a marriage so efficiently splits love and physical passion that the love that remains is substantial and real. What made the marriage of Harold Nicolson and Vita Sackville-West extraordinary, apart from their culture, wealth and green fingers, was the intensity of her lesbian loves. To balance two kinds of deep love is a rare feat. Splitting love and sex is as old as keeping a wife and a mistress, but harder if both passions are powerful. She was not an innocent bride in 1913 as the diaries published by her son after her death reveal:

> It never struck me as wrong that I should be more or less engaged to Harold, and at the same time very much in love with Rosamund. The fact is that I regarded Harold far more as a playfellow than in any other light. Our relationship was so fresh, so intellectual, so unphysical, that I never thought of him in that aspect at all . . . although I was very fond of him, I was passionately in love with herself – I use the word 'passionately' on purpose. It was passion that used to make my head swim sometimes, even in the daytime, but we never made love.

On another occasion she wrote:

> I separate my loves into two halves; Harold, who is unalterable, perennial and *best*: there has never been anything but absolute purity in my love for Harold, just as there has never been anything but absolute bright purity in his nature. And on the other hand stands my perverted nature, which loved and tyrannized over Rosamund and ended by deserting her without one heart-pang, and which now is linked irremediably with Violet.

Her lesbian passions subsided during early marriage:

> For sheer joy of companionship I should think the years that followed were unparalleled or at least unsurpassed. One side of my nature was so dormant that I believed it would never revive. I was really gentle, self-sacrificing, chaste; I was *too* good, if anything, because it made me intolerant of the frailties of other people. (Now, I feel I could forgive anyone anything.) We were a sort of byword for happiness and union. We never tired of one

another! How rescued I felt from everything that was vicious and violent! Harold was like a sunny harbour to me. It was all open, frank, certain; and although I never knew the physical passion I had felt for Rosamund, I didn't really miss it. This lasted intact for about four and a half years.

The crisis came when her lover, Violet, married. So stunned was Vita that she determined to break up the marriage before it was consummated and confronted the couple in their hotel in Paris two days after the wedding. She took Violet to her hotel, 'treated her savagely, I made love to her, I had her, I didn't care, I only wanted to hurt Denys . . .' Violet told Denys that she had meant to run away with Vita instead of marrying him, and that she did not love him. That night, while Vita dined at the Ritz, she saw from the open window of her room Violet watching her, with Denys sobbing in the room behind her.

The two women left for Greece, Vita in her male disguise as 'Julian', trousered, smoking, but they came home again. Vita stayed married to Harold and Violet to Denys until death did them part.

Women in those days had the cover of a repressive society. They expected to get married, and become engaged without a kiss. Their families would have been more alert to any genealogical than sexual incompatibility. Like the newlywed Franklin Delano Roosevelts about the same era (Vita married Harold in 1913, Eleanor married Franklin in 1905), the wives got pregnant almost immediately, and soon again after that.

In letters published in 1979, Eleanor Roosevelt is revealed as having loved Lorena Hickok, her close friend and companion of thirty years, to the point of writing in December 1933:

Dear, I've been trying today to bring back your face – to remember just how you look. Funny how even the dearest face will fade away in time. Most clearly I remember your eyes, with a kind of reassuring smile in them, and the feeling of that soft spot just northeast of the corner of your mouth against my lips. I wonder what we'll do when we méet – what we'll say. Well, I'm rather proud of us, aren't you? I think we've done rather well.

116

A few weeks earlier she wrote from the White House: 'Dear one, and so you think they gossip about us, well they must at least think we stand separations rather well! I am always so much more optimistic than you are – I suppose because I care so little what "they say".' And, later: 'One cannot hide things in this world, can one? How lucky you are not a man!'

A Victorian kind of delicacy prevailed in comment by the press when the letters were made public. The venerability of Mrs Roosevelt made speculation about her sex life far more uncomfortable than anything that accompanied earlier revelations about extramarital affairs of her husband. Those had simply put the former First Family into the tradition of naughty old dog and the saintly mother who isn't interested in sex anyway. About his late mother's letters, Franklin Roosevelt, Jr, her literary executor, commented that effusive expressions of endearment were the convention in correspondence among women of that time brought up on the Brontës and Jane Austen.

Even today lesbian women can be quick with the reasons why they stay in a marriage: 'I don't think he could manage by himself' or 'I would find it hard to leave him because he would miss me' or 'He would miss the children' or 'I love the guy'. These are the same excuses that the wives of gay men use for not walking out, with the difference that the lesbian wives feel stronger as individuals because they have made the break for sexual freedom. From San Francisco a lesbian writes: 'I thought I had given up the love that dare not speak its name when I moved to the Coast. Next month I am going to visit my lesbian love in Saskatchewan. I'm head over heels in love with her (head over whose heels I ask). But you can tell people that I don't feel at all trapped in my heterosexual marriage.'

Most lesbians seem to get a divorce and strike out on their own. Their way of living is very much like that of other women, and much different from that of gay men. Lesbians are not female versions of male homosexuals. There is a gulf between the two groups that the gay rights organizations are trying to bridge, but the facts of gay life are against them. The sexes are very different. According to the Kinsey Institute study, most of the women reported having had fewer than ten female partners in their adult lives. They do not like sex with strangers and virtually never pay for it. Most prefer stable relationships. Three-quarters, the Kinsey Institute found, were living with a long-term partner. They shared expenses and housework. They were less worried about preserving eternal youth than are most male gays and heterosexual women. Their recognition that they were lesbian was usually based on a love affair, after which the thought of finding someone permanent became the most important thing in their life. The 'casual' relationship lasted from one to three months, not for just one night. Lesbians' only 'male' characteristic, according to the research of Saghir and Robins, psychiatrists at the Washington University of St Louis Medical School, is a high tendency towards alcoholism. They do not play roles, the team found, and resent bitterly the popular idea that the lesbian couple is always divided into 'butch' and 'femme', like Sister George and Childie in *The Killing of Sister George*.

There is one other way in which male gays are very different from females: they have more money. Lesbians might well complain of economic discrimination. In San Francisco, the Kinsey study reported, landlords do not like lesbians as tenants, while in contrast they welcome homosexual men, with their skills at interior decoration and unfettered incomes to pour into it. Advertisements for condominiums and credit card clubs catering to 'the gay lifestyle' are not addressed to lesbian women, who, with children or without, usually have lower incomes, who are careless about dress and décor and who live not in the centre of cities, but in the suburbs. The celebrated 'gay lifestyle' is largely for bachelor men.

118

9

Case Unsolved

He kept his coat on, watching the other men, all of whom were gay, sitting with their wives, at a meeting for people with homosexual or bisexual partners. He was that breed rarely spotted – the husband of a lesbian. 'I'm here,' he said, the words hardly escaping his clenched teeth, 'to find out what makes a woman . . . what can come over a woman . . . that she can leave her home and husband just because . . . of some woman she's met!'

Did he have any children?

'Five!'

He stayed and stared, saying nothing, learning nothing. He went back to the home he is trying to keep together in the hope that his wife, whom he sees as 'mesmerized' by a nurse, will return to her senses and her family.

It would not be accurate to say that men who find out that their wives are lesbian have suffered a wounding blow to their male pride. The whole concept of manhood links it to competing with other men. To lose a woman to a woman is not threatening but bewildering. The most common initial reaction is complete, utter stupefaction, then curiosity, then denial, and according to temperament and class, rage.

The husband who blurted out, 'Can I watch?' was expressing what is well known to pornographers: that men are turned on by the idea of two women together. (Once when the author was being shown around a prison in Wales, a guard explained the official policy on pin-ups: 'We don't allow anything really pornographic.' He spoke standing with his back to a cell wall on which was pasted a picture of two nude women fingering each other.) Sex between women in the male view, as in Queen Victoria's, does not count as sex, and can make a nice preliminary to the Real Thing. This phenomenon enrages lesbians. They report that many a husband, when given the news about his wife's lover, has suggested a threesome. Some married women agree, to preserve the marriage, but their women lovers will not put up with the triangle for long. For men who know lesbians only from a distance, the thrill is augmented by the belief (comparable to the conviction of sexy fag hags) that these women would not prefer their own sex if they only had a few hours with a real man – guess who? If the women are good-looking and not butch, men see lesbians as a challenge. For many lesbians, the expectation of this rote response makes men seem all the more terrifying. One woman said her fear of straight men was so intense that she could only talk with men at her gay club. Her fear was not helped when she put a notice in a gay newspaper saying she wanted to start a local branch of a lesbian organization. She received seventy obscene phone calls from men, many of them wanting a date. 'I could have started a bordello,' she said.

The counterpart of the gay's understanding wife is the denying husband. He just blocks it out. One husband used to drive his lesbian wife to visit her friend and wait outside in the car until she came out, then drive her home. About what they might be doing in there, he kept his mind a blank.

Otto Preminger has joked about life in Hollywood where 'a nice lesbian relationship, the most common thing in the world, and very easy to arrange, doesn't threaten the marriage'. Many husbands would like to believe that, and in times past, a *ménage à trois*, with a woman friend of the family as a permanent houseguest, caused no comment whatsoever. If today's husband wants to keep his lesbian wife, he may find the number of a lesbian organization in a gay or counter-culture newspaper and give it a call. He will explain considerately that his wife is too shy to make the call herself, but that he is an open, helpful man and he wants the marriage to continue. Could the group find his wife some sort of lover or friend to appease this little desire of hers so that life will all be normal again? (The answer he gets is not what he wanted: that lesbianism is very real to his wife, that it won't go away and if he wants to show his understanding, to put her on the line and let her speak for herself).

The perplexity of a husband is understandable because his wife seemed to change character overnight. When he asks her what has happened, unless she has become a lesbian out of feminist fervour, she probably will not be able to explain how she discovered her homosexuality any better than the teacher who said: 'Just walking around the corner and bumping into somebody. As simple as that.' If it is that simple, a husband will ask, why do you have to move out and get a divorce? Why not just do it? One man, a doctor, is still mystified over the circumstances of his wife's desertion: she had never had any homosexual experience, the woman she left to live with was ten years older, had also been married, had had lovers and never a trace of lesbianism, yet his wife not only walked out, but left her baby girl behind. 'I cannot conceive of there being any woman for whom I would give up my child,' he says. 'How could a woman do that?' (He has custody; his wife did not seek it.) But that was not the reason for the divorce, he added. The marriage was breaking up anyway.

Why, why, why? The lesbian will answer that a man does not understand the completeness of the relationship between two women, that he thinks of it in terms of schoolgirl crushes instead of violent orgasmic passion on a sweat-stained bed. But the average husband will walk away, like Woody Allen in the film *Manhattan*, find himself a *bone fide* heterosexual girl and file his lesbian ex-wife under 'case unsolved'. He does not want to talk about it. He has other things on his mind.

Until he begins living with or marries the other woman, that is. Then he is a couple, a family unit again, and fortified with a female, will fight in the courts, or as this case from the British lesbian newspaper, *Sappho*, reports, in the kitchen:

MARY. 'Then her husband comes back to discuss the children. We asked him to call, because everything was getting out of proportion. I visited Sue's home for the meeting. So he

121

arrives with his girlfriend after the pubs shut at 11.30 at night. She was paralytic. He was in no way. His feelings had built up and he hadn't had a chance to let go. Then the fight broke out. His girlfriend fought Sue. I got up to stop it. He twisted my neck; he kicked Sue in the eye. He went berserk and grabbed me. The kids came screaming downstairs. We were all on top of each other. It was the worst night of my life. We got them out. He went to the police to say we'd beaten them up. Not a mark on him. Sue had scratched his girl friend's face – '

SUE. 'When they left – two in the morning – she yelled, "Bloody Lesbians!"'

MARY. 'The police came round to see us. They couldn't do nothing. It was domestic.'

To many people, marriages between a lesbian and a homosexual may seem made in heaven. In reality, they are contracted far less often than is imagined. The Kinsey San Francisco study found them rarely reported. Saghir and Robins, the Washington and St Louis psychiatrists who have studied female homosexuality, found that one out of three lesbians who had married had chosen a man whom they either knew or suspected to be a homosexual. These marriages were no more successful than those to heterosexual men, almost always ending in divorce. It is almost as if at least one partner in a marriage has to be minimally sexually interested in the other for it to have any life at all. Out-and-out marriages of convenience, whether for social cover or for purposes of immigration or inheritance, do not seem to take hold. The homosexual man mentioned earlier who married a lesbian because 'the normal would produce children and the non-normal would not' found that his wife kept her marriage vows just as long as he kept his, for seven years. But one night in Greece, on holiday, they had a terrible fight. He walked out, met a man in a bar and went off with him to Morocco. He telephoned his wife from there. He did not come home for six weeks. When he got home, he found that she had resumed her lesbianism. He moved out. She now has a steady lover who lives three doors away. The children think they have an extra aunt. Unconscious lesbianism, of course, is one explanation of why women think they can put up with a husband's acknowledged gayness. When the husband decides at last to go gay, the wife realizes that she can do the same.

A divorced lesbian sits amid the unpacked books and crockery and flaking walls of her new flat. It is in a rundown district in Cambridge, Massachusetts, where academic families foolishly do not dare to move. Lean, tanned and black-haired, a well-mannered woman in her late thirties, she is wearing shorts, a sleeveless T-shirt and the regulation no bra. Her daughter, who is eleven, is away visiting her father. For the summer she has organized her working desk, a bulletin board stuck with printed notices, postcards, and snapshots of herself in the nude. One shows an open crotch. This woman is from southern Minnesota, where she went to a small Midwestern Lutheran college and married as her family expected her to, just after graduation. From adolescence, she knew she was attracted to women but had not put any label on the feeling, nor taken any action. She dated men students.

'I had slept with some of them and was semi-engaged to one. My best friend was Jim. I was closer to him than to any of the women – they were all competing with each other for men. I did have some close lesbian friends and I saw what a hell of a burden it was. A lot of them drank a lot. The only fellow that was appealing didn't seem as much of a trap as the others. He was gay then. He asked me to marry him. We discussed it openly. In our marriage deal, his starting point was that he was very unhappy and wanted to lead a heterosexual life. He wanted to see a therapist with a specific purpose and wound up seeing the same person I was seeing.

'At first he was absolutely frigid. The idea of sleeping with a woman was – ugh. But it was something that he wanted to change. I took it on as a kind of interesting challenge. It helped me. Most of the men I knew thought of themselves first, second and only. In bed he did things other than watch his own reaction. I hadn't done anything about

123

being attracted to women. We got so that for both of us it was quite enjoyable.'

The marriage deteriorated after their daughter was born, after she had worked to push him through graduate school and they had moved to Cambridge. He was teaching at MIT. They were disagreeing about a lot of things, money and childcare responsibilities, and one day he invited her for a summit talk at the MIT Faculty Club. He suggested 'open marriage' which was much in vogue at the time – 'that what we should do is take other lovers, men or women, it doesn't matter'. It was obvious from the clothes he was buying – the tightest trousers she'd ever seen, shirts designed to be worn open, tiny, bright underpants – in which direction he was proposing to open their marriage.

At that time there was a woman for whom she'd been aware of an attraction. After a month's hard thinking she told her husband she would pursue that relationship. He did not believe her but she did. The woman responded and they 'became involved, sexually and emotionally'. For about six months, she and her husband tried to make the marriage work, then gave it up as a lost cause. That was several years ago. She has a new lover now. They will stay together. 'This is the best relationship I've ever been involved in, a constantly questioning, moving relationship.' The new sexual identity is the right one, it seems, for both husband and wife.

10

In Front of the Children

An army officer resigned his commission and divorced his wife when he fell in love with another man. He got a good job as a systems analyst, and he and his lover have been together for five years. As far as they can see, they will stay together for the rest of their lives. They have jobs, a home, lots of friends, mainly stable couples like themselves, homosexual and heterosexual. Had he any children from his former marriage? He suddenly finds it hard to speak. Tears fill his eyes and will not stop coming.

'No. I wish to God I did. That is the one thing I'm sorry about, that I desperately miss. It's even worse because I'm the end of the line for my family. I'm the only son of an only son. My father kept his toys for me, and I'd been keeping my toys for . . .'

He believes he would be a good father. He likes children. As one who openly switched from straight to gay, he has witnessed the full range of reactions of all his friends. It was children, and mothers with children, who were the most understanding. One little girl, after visiting the two men in their home, asked her mother, 'Do they love each other? Well, that's okay then.'

Talking to homosexuals who want children is to be deluged with the cold water of common sense. How could it be otherwise? Why should sexual preference have anything to do with the desire for children? That producing a child does not guarantee love for the other parent is obvious enough. To the vast majority of society, however, it is by no means obvious that homosexuals can even feel the normal urges to have and to love a child. They are seen as too narcissistic to want a dependant, and to be positively revolted by children. It is equally true that wanting children is incompatible with the gay political ethos. On the estate of parenthood the childless gay man can be even more scathing than the radical feminist. He scorns the muddy sentimentality of parents, with their thinly disguised desire for immortality in the shape of little clones to represent them in the next century. The flamboyantly effeminate hairdresser is simply scandalized by the thought: 'Madame, the homosexual is by nature promiscuous. He should have nothing to do with bringing up children.' But these views represent only half the picture.

If there is a continuum of sexual orientation, so too there is a range of feelings about family life. Many married male homosexuals are 'bi' in the sense of having equally passionate desires to have a homosexual love life and to have children of their own. There is a group for whom children were the overwhelming motive for marriage. Fear of losing the children is the biggest barrier to coming out. One man, aged thirty-five, who has been thrown out by his wife because of his homosexuality, wrote to say:

> Our beautiful baby girl was born in 1966 and the news of her birth was, and still remains, the most thrilling moment of my entire life. Even the birth of my son could not surpass that first feeling of bringing a life, a new life, into the world for the first time.

The child-hating queen is real enough. When the fastidious bachelor played by Clifton Webb in the film *Sitting Pretty* tips the cereal bowl over the head of the bawling toddler, he acts for the overgrown child in us all who cannot bear the mess and the noise and who wants to be the only child in the room. What is more, many homosexuals live in elegant surroundings and want to keep them that way. A mother can understand the King's Road antique dealer who told her and her child to leave because the child was munching a meringue. 'Not in my shop, you don't,' he said.

Like other men, male homosexuals have absorbed the primitive concept of children as wealth and a proof of virility. One divorced gay man, totally committed to the gay lifestyle, keeps photographs of his handsome children around his flat to display to the pick-ups whom he brings home. He wants to show off what he's got. Almost every homosexual father interviewed for this book brought out

126

pictures of his children.

Most said that if starting out now, they would not marry, but that fatherhood was one of the pleasures they would not have missed. 'I can't regret my marriage, because that would mean regretting my children. They are the joy of my life', said a social worker.

Hallam Tennyson, the great-grandson of the poet, a writer and broadcaster, gives talks at homosexual meetings in London in tandem with his daughter Ros. He is divorced. 'My children are to me the miracle of all time. Ros and Jonny are straight but, perhaps because I'm gay, they have a natural identification with the handicapped of society. I loved bringing them up. My nostalgia now is not for my own childhood but for theirs: it was one of the best times of my life.'

If, as so many gay men confirm, they knew well before the age of ten that they were gay, it means that they grew up with the suspicion that they might be excluded from fatherhood. When they achieve it, it may therefore be doubly valuable to them. If, as much psychoanalytic theory says, an absent father plays some part in causing some adults to prefer their own sex erotically, then some may want to reproduce the home life they think they should have had. However, gay people, once they are parents, are no more theoretical than straight parents. They have produced the children. They love them.

Lesbian mother love is less easily discounted. Mother love is so idealized that no great stretch of the heterosexual imagination is required to believe that a homosexual woman feels it too, and the ferocity with which a lesbian fights for custody should convince any doubters. A mother is a mother. Who cares what she does in bed, after she has got up four times in the night? Motherhood desexualizes.

The Italian picture weekly, *Oggi*, put on its cover the 44-year-old Ursula Andress with her new-born son, at the breast seen through its nursing bra. It was the subject that Italians, from Old Masters to *paparazzi*, love: sexpot become Mama. You can't have evil thoughts about *her*.

*

127

The children grow up. How to tell the children the facts of their parents' life? Should they be told at all? In what words, and when? There is nothing in Dr Spock for guidance. All that gay people can do is ask each other. Many hope the children will simply find it out for themselves and many get their wish. A journalist tells how his daughter learned: 'She saw me coming out of The Champion in Notting Hill Gate. "That's a gay pub, isn't it?" she said. I said yes, and that was that.' A lesbian headmistress found reticence the best policy: 'When I met the woman I'm now living with, it struck me like a bump on the head. From then on I didn't spend a night at home unless I absolutely had to. My daughter, she's now twenty-six, said, "You two are like a pair of teenagers the way you go on." But she said outright that she didn't want to know any more about it. One lesbian I know has a daughter twelve years old who knows all the details, but I'm the wrong generation.'

Another woman did not have to do any telling because: 'My sister-in-law called me a filthy lesbian one day. I didn't know my little girl had heard. When I went to her school on parents' night, the teacher told me, laughing, that when they were talking about religion, my daughter had said, "I know what religion we are. We're lesbians." The teacher never dreamed it was true – because I was married.'

Those who choose secrecy believe they are preserving their children's respect: 'My only regret as a homosexual is that my children might reject me. It's a constant nightmare.' The familiar generalization works for this problem – men and women handle it differently. The woman tells the kids; the men do not. The question homosexual parents ought to put to themselves, however, is whether they like to believe they know the truth about their own parents' lives. Would they like to know whether one of their parents had been married before or had had an illegitimate child? These are common family secrets. If they place a high value on knowing the truth about their own background, they might conclude that their children have a right to the same.

The parent who accepts his homosexuality will probably

tell his children directly. A father with twin boys: 'I told them when they were fifteen. I told them bluntly and then explained what it was all about. They wept, then they coped. They were warm and accepting. Now, ten years later, one is gay, one is not. I've shepherded the gay one through his first love at sixteen.' There are many accounts of similar moments of revelation in the gay press, which boil down to the child saying: 'You're still my father/mother, aren't you?' They take the news much better than wives, and why not? Children are not interested in their parents' sex life. Even as adults, they keep a protective amnesia about what their parents probably had to do to bring them into the world.

Once they do know that their parent has faced the problem of a taboo kind of sexuality, they may feel easier bringing up their own problems. One mother, a social worker, who ventured cautiously, 'You can keep men, I like women,' heard her daughters crying in dismay, 'You're not turning lezzie on us, are you, Mum?' A little while later the older daughter came and confessed that she was having difficulty with her boyfriend. 'Frank can't get it up, Mum. Maybe you ought to have a talk with him.'

If one of the pleasant surprises about children is how forgiving they are, homosexual parents are doubly blessed. A grown son teased his mother when he applied for a security clearance for work in Australia: 'I don't know how I'll get my security clearance, Mum,' he said, 'with your record.'

The comfortable picture of all-accepting children is finding its way into the sociological literature and is overall probably true. Children will accept what they cannot change; they love a parent who loves them. But to pretend that the news of the parent's homosexuality does not cause them a lot of inner turmoil about their own sexual identity is wishful thinking. The following story from an American mother sounds more realistic.

'The first thing I said [to a six-year-old boy] was that Bob and I were still his parents and intended to be still his parents, but that the person most important to me emotionally – the primary love I felt for an adult – was for this woman, and that that was not the way people usually did it. And that Bob wanted to direct those same kind of feelings towards men, and that this was not something that most people did.

'My life with women didn't bother him. He shrugged and said, "That's okay," and he went on with his life. But he had a lot of turmoil about his father. He started stuttering if he knew he was going to visit Bob, and it would last for a month after. Like a good mother, I carried him off to a therapist, who, after play sessions and whatever they do, conveyed to me that he had a lot of worries about himself – that stuttering was an indication of how he feels about his father.

'Now that he is twelve, he and I spend a lot of time talking about his own sexuality. "I know I am free to make up my mind," he says, "and I like girls." His friends are already going out on dates and last vacation he had a little girlfriend for a couple of days. A few years ago he had a lot of questions about Bob's gayness. "What does this mean for me?" he would ask. His therapist's opinion is that he was tossing this around in his own mind and was coming down on the side of being heterosexual, that the question of being gay would recur for him but his choices weren't tortured . . . and that he was heterosexual.

'What do I want for him? I can't put it in a hetero–homosexual context. An intimate mutual relationship, I guess. If I were making a value judgement, and considered what the rest of society thinks about gay relationships – that they're superficial, lacking intimacy – I wouldn't want that for him. Life would be easier for him as a heterosexual but it really doesn't matter to me.'

For politically active gay people, telling the children is mandatory. Even the most liberated, however, when their children are small, are confronted with the problems of the bedroom, and somewhere a judge may be watching. For conservatives the solution is to put the lover in a temporary bed and pretend he is just a roommate. Some lesbian couples too are meticulous, maintaining separate bedrooms or moving to a couch when the children come. For others, such manoeuvres are the height of prurience. As with nudity, they cannot see what all the fuss is about: a Manhattan doctor says, 'My daughters, eleven and nine, adore my current lover. He is a very beautiful youth, Antonio, and bright, a dancer. He loves them. We have two bedrooms. When they're staying with us, they come and crawl in with us in the morning.'

But is a gay parent good for the children? The question splits into two unanswerable parts: What is a good parent? What causes homosexuality?

For some years, homosexual thinkers have been at war with the psychoanalysts. While even to try to state their opposing views risks distortion (a risk which the next chapter takes) the psychoanalytic view on which courts and social agencies base their decisions is that the child needs two parents, one parent of each sex, in order to progress to heterosexual maturity. The parent of the same sex is necessary as a model. The other parent is necessary as the first love object of the opposite sex. Lacking either, the child will grow up with a distorted perspective which may express itself in homosexuality.

So much for the theory. There are popular fears, widely held at all levels, including the bench, which also work against the homosexual's claim to be a good parent. They are:

1. That homosexuality is contagious and that a parent will pass it on to a child.

2. That homosexuals are sexually attracted to children. A child living in a homosexual home, therefore, is in danger of being molested by the parent's partner, or even the parent.

3. That a house headed by a homosexual couple is inherently unhealthy an environment for a child.

4. That a child will suffer ridicule from other children and the community.

So controversial have these issues become in recent years, with gay liberation and custody fights by lesbian mothers, that a number of research projects have focused on children of homosexual (usually lesbian) parents. The results have been all that the homosexual could wish. No evidence has turned up that the children of homosexuals are more mixed-up, disturbed, or, for that matter, homosexual, than the children of divorced parents in general. Second-generation homosexuals are rare.

The first thorough psychological study of children of lesbian mothers was published in 1976 by Dr Martha Kirkpatrick of the University of California at Los Angeles medical school. While the twenty children in her study did have problems, they were the familiar ones associated with divorce. The children worried about whether they had caused their parents to break up and whether they would lose either parent in the future. There was no sign of any one of them becoming homosexual, sexually confused or disoriented.

The same finding – no difference between the offspring of homosexual and heterosexual parents – was published by Dr Pepper Schwartz, a sociologist from the University of Washington. It was based on a large national study of couples, including lesbians with custody.

Perhaps the most interesting and unexpected result has come from the work of Dr Richard Green of the State University of New York. One of his studies was a psychiatric evaluation of thirty-seven children being raised by female homosexuals or by transsexual parents who had had a surgical change of sex. Of these, thirty-six did not show any sign of confused gender identity in their choice of toys, games or friends. In other words, they knew whether they were male or female. In all of the teenagers sexual orientation was developing in the appropriate pattern. Dr Green refuted the belief that the sexual style of the parents is the only factor in the child's psychological development. It appears that the child takes his or her sexual model from the whole society, not just from his parents or their lovers. A boy learns what a man is like from watching television and from going to school, as well as from his father. If maleness is what he identifies himself with, he will take his clues from everywhere.

Dr Green reported that the children either experienced

no teasing or had shrugged it off. A twelve-year-old boy told him that a schoolmate had called his mother butch because of the way she dressed. He ignored it and was not teased again. Reflecting, the boy said, 'She can be anything she wants, as long as she's still my mother.'

Many childcare experts and sociologists agree: it is the quality of the love and attention given a child that determines whether the child grows up emotionally well-adjusted, not the sexual tastes of the parent. In sum, as Dr Spock put it (in a letter written for the National Gay Task Force), questions about the parents' right to visit a child or to have custody should not be decided on sexual orientation, but on observable factors like the parents' devotion to their children, their good sense in managing them, their general ethical standards and their children's love for them.

As for the charge that homosexuals are people who are attracted to children, criminal conviction figures dispel it quickly. In cases of sexual abuse, female children were victims nearly twice as often as male children. Paedophiles, people whose erotic preference is for children, tend to be heterosexual.

As for the accusation that homosexuals are proselytizers for homosexuality, gay parents answer with one voice: 'I would not mind if my children were homosexual, but life would be easier for them if they were not. Above all, I don't want them to go through the guilt and deception that I did.'

These questions are hardly academic. They arise in many court cases involving a homosexual parent. Observers report that in the ordinary process of divorce, the issue of homosexuality does not come up in court, for there is no need. It arises only when someone wants to hurt someone, or when a grandparent or a new wife wants to have the child, and petitions for custody or visiting rights to be altered.

The homosexual community has coined a word to describe people, especially judges, who are unsympathetic: homophobic. Yet this emotive label, while sometimes true, is often unfair. For some time, judges in family cases, who have learned the lessons of Freud and Bowlby, have tried to make difficult custody decisions on the principle of the best interest of the child. With so little evidence available to counteract the stereotypes of the past, they have had no choice but to trust the conventional wisdom which for decades has interpreted the best interest as living, if possible, in a home where there is a parent of each sex, and which has looked with suspicion on same-sex pairs. So much research remains to be done, such as studying the long-range effects on children living with lesbian couples and observing the kinds of marriages the children eventually make. Can two women bring up a boy? Some doctors are reluctant to see artificial insemination provided for lesbian mothers in case the child is male. Some lesbians have their own doubts and go to Big Brother Associations or similar agencies to find role models for their sons. Which view is right – Juno's in Sean O'Casey's *Juno and the Paycock*, who in answer to her unwed daughter's complaint, 'My poor baby, he'll have no father,' says, 'He'll have something better – two mothers'? Or Woody Allen's in *Manhattan*? Playing a father whose wife has gone lesbian, he says, 'My son has two mothers. Most people I know have trouble surviving one mother.'

There is no way to resolve these doubts at present. The research results, however encouraging, are based on samples too small to carry the weight the homosexual community is placing on them.

Gay groups everywhere advise the lesbian mother seeking custody to brace herself for a fight. The first rule is to find a sympathetic lawyer – one who has handled a homosexual custody case before, and one who is not visibly homosexual. As judges place great reliance on professional experts, these too must be chosen with care. 'One expert we used sounded fine when we spoke to him on the phone,' said a woman legal worker from the Portland, Oregon, Community Law Project. 'But he came into court with five rings on each hand, his hair slicked back, wearing a silver suit that shone under the lights. I thought I was going to die. We had simply never thought to counsel the expert.'

The lover's appearance counts even more. She will almost certainly be called into court and subjected to a worse grilling than either parent. A checklist of questions for consideration prepared by the American Lesbian Mother Custody Center asks: 'Are you prepared to make a conventional appearance for both your child and yourself, i.e., clothes, hair etc? What limitations on your political personal activities are you willing to accept? If you don't believe anyone knows about your being gay, how certain are you? Do you live with your lover? Go to the bars?'

Judges, it is suggested, are by no means immune from the sexual titillation that many men find in the thought of lesbianism. They will press for detail upon detail of what lesbians do in bed. The suggested tactic is to arrange for an expert witness to answer the explicit sexual questions. Still, lesbians should be prepared for a rough ride.

The London-based lesbian organization, Sappho, warns, 'However gentle, honest and charming and loving your lover might be, the other side will make her out to be an evil, randy seducer who dominates the mother totally. However stable and loving your relationship, the other side may attempt to make out that your life together is nothing more than a series of sexual adventures (in front of the child) in a house strewn with "appliances".'

This ordeal may prove too much for the lover; she may balk at the request to appear in court or to switch to separate bedrooms to please the judge. 'Let's hope,' says Sappho, 'that you don't have to make the decision about which is the most important – her or the child. You could end up by losing both . . . The odds are against you. We would be wrong not to tell you this. We all thought we had good cases.' In consolation, Sappho offers a piece of advice that holds just as true for the thousands of divorced fathers who lose custody and believe they have lost their children for ever: 'If you do lose, the only option is to maintain as good a relationship as possible with your children and see them as often as you can. No court can stop your children coming to live with you of their own free will as soon as they are old enough to get on a train or a bus and as soon as they are old enough to decide for themselves (and not have grown-ups deciding for them) what they want to do!'

For a long while, a lesbian mother had virtually no chance of winning custody. In 1970, according to the Lesbian Mothers National Defense Fund in Seattle, only 1 per cent of contested custody cases were won. Today the mothers are winning in 15 per cent of the cases. The trend is visible even in more conservative Britain. The change of policy is a victory for common sense and realism. None of the research studies nor the lesbian campaigns have altered the fact that a home with two loving parents is best for a child. But the rise in divorce has meant that the old ideal has had to be abandoned as a practical guide. The one-parent family is commonplace – one out of eight British children lives in one. The reconstituted family, particularly the home that a father makes with his new wife, looks less cosy than it did – not an obvious better alternative for a child than living with his or her natural mother. Against this background, the lesbian mother's claim to keep her child, and the research findings that in many cases she is a better mother – more assertive and self-reliant – than the divorced mother looking for another man, is increasingly defeating the opposition.

So flexible has the practice become in some liberal states that in Denver, Colorado, in 1979, the court awarded custody of a girl to the lover of a lesbian mother who had died. Donna Levy and the child's mother had lived together as lovers for thirteen years and had brought up the child, Betty, born during that time. The two women later split up but Donna remained close to Betty and saw her often. Then Betty's mother committed suicide, leaving a note asking that Donna should have custody. However, Betty's aunt and her husband fought for custody and won it temporarily. Then they separated and the judge, a woman, awarded custody to Donna.

'Donna's sexual preference has not affected the child in the past and is not related to her ability to parent the child,' declared Judge Orrelle Weeks. 'Her strengths as a parent to the child are her sensitivity, her ability to empathize with the child, her warmth and her dependability.'

Men have a harder time. A vindictive ex-wife can even deprive them of visiting rights or have the child adopted by her new husband if she chooses to fight on the gay issue. A gay father winning custody from a straight mother really would be news. Even on visiting rights, judges often ask that the child be protected from the 'lifestyle'.

'My lawyer told me,' said a New York lawyer, ' "You'd better not take the children out to Fire Island." "Then we've got a problem," I said, "because I've just bought a house out there." So the first year, I wouldn't have them there over a weekend. Now their mother is more relaxed and I have them when I like. I'm discreet. I don't let them go to the disco. Otherwise my lover and I live our lives. We share a double bed, yes, we do. The children accept it. I've already told my oldest daughter about heterosexual sex. If she wants to discuss what I do in bed now, I will. I express affection to Harvey in the ordinary way. As long as the kids get their dinner, they will accept you. The younger you start them, the easier they accept it. It's perfectly natural.'

One sociological study concludes that gay fathers do a better job than fathers who are secret homosexuals. Those men are constantly scolded by their wives for not spending enough time with the children – with good reason. Their double life takes time away from home. Men who become publicly gay and leave their wives report 'fathering to be more important and more fulfilling now that they are away from their marriage'.

As gay fathers come out, more and more of today's homosexual lovers are having to play the part of stepparent. They are faced with many of the familiar problems: how much to discipline the child, how to hide their resentment of this intruder. The child is a constant reminder of the partner's sexual intercourse with someone else, and a constant drain on money and attention, someone who makes a lot of work and who often arrives just when they want to relax. The child can carry stories back to the other parent – who may be looking for tales of homosexual hanky-panky to take to court to plead for a cessation of visiting rights.

A businessman took his lover's twelve-year-old daughter out to lunch. 'Will you adopt me?' she asked. 'But you *have* a mother and a father,' he pointed out. She was disappointed. What she wanted, he reasoned, was to be related to his mother of whom she was very fond. She really wanted the grandmother.

That part of the homosexual world that does not like children is unlikely to get involved with a gay daddy. As among lesbians, there is a gulf between the two groups, those who are parents and those who are not. Some newly gay men try to become closet fathers but the evidence is hard to conceal. 'He saw the toys and that was that. Even the thought that I had touched a woman defiled me in his eyes.' Obviously, the man who is willing to set up house with a gay father will not be in that category and therefore may be hiding his own envy.

'My lover has never been married. He is at an age when he would like to father a child – he's twenty-nine. My response is that I was not sure I could accept that burden. I appreciate that I'm not being entirely fair because I want him to be a stepfather to my children.' (Or stepmother, perhaps?) 'Yeah, I make him out to be the heavy – the stepmother. He makes sure they keep their room good and tidy when they visit.'

One lesbian mother, in contrast, tries to keep a distance between her partner and her young son: 'I don't ask her to babysit or discipline him. One thing I have not looked for is a replacement parent. What I would like is that the two of them like each other and find a way to get along with each other. They do.'

For the homosexual, stepparenting is one way to vicarious parenthood. Many straight couples are deciding that the children of a previous marriage are all the children they want. Second families are expensive and many remarried men have neither the money nor the inclination to start a new family. If the second wife has a career she does not want to interrupt, she may find a way to vent her motherly feelings on the stepchild. This quasi-parenthood is probably easier for the gay men if the stepchild is female, for there are compensations for young girls whose fathers go off with another man rather than another woman; they remain Daddy's girl for life.

If she does not blame him for the break-up of her parents' marriage, the daughter can probably get along well with her father's lover. Where is the research on how well girls get on with their mother's lesbian partner? It would be surprising if some of the traditional stepdaughter-stepmother jealousy did not surface.

Many gay men feel that nurturing is something they are good at. They may be content to express it through the classic detours – teaching, scouting, social work and religion, becoming shepherds of other people's children. But for some, this will not suffice.

What are homosexual men supposed to do with their wish to be parents? Lesbians have no problem and are easily turning to artificial insemination to acquire a child all their own.

Adoption, if they are a settled couple and living in a tolerant environment, is one answer for men. When Alvin Toffler wrote *Future Shock* in 1970, he was trying to shock. One prediction for the future techno-society was that there might even begin to be families based on homosexual 'marriage' with partners adopting children. The future has arrived. Adoption by homosexuals has already begun. Such adoptions in law are made by one person only, for homosexuals, not being married, cannot present themselves as a married couple. When the news is given out, it gets a lot of attention, as in June 1979, in the *New York Times*: 'Approval Given for Homosexual to Adopt a Boy'. A homosexual minister, the Rev. John Kuiper of Catskill, New York, was granted permanent custody of the thirteen-year-old boy he had been caring for. Mr Kuiper, pastor of the Good News Metropolitan Community Church in Albany, a mainly homosexual church, publicly announced that he was living with a forty-year-old man in a homosexual relationship. He had discovered he was homosexual, he said, after he had been granted temporary permission to adopt. The family court investigated the home and the school and sent its report to the Green County family court. Judge James Battista said: 'The reverend is providing a good home, the boy loves his adoptive father and wants to be with him. Who knows in this world of ours? You do the best you can and hope it works out.' Judge Battista assumed that some people would be critical but from his perspective he saw a far from ideal world: 'The man doesn't beat his son, and when you look at all the cases of child abuse you get from so-called straights, you gasp for words.'

The boy, who had been shunted from institutional home to institutional home all his life, was delighted. 'I knew I'd stay with my dad,' he said. 'My dad has explained everything to me, and it's OK. It's his decision.' All agree that the boy is heterosexual. That is fine with Reverend Kuiper; he would like grandchildren.

Two clergymen in Los Angeles in 1979 have probably come closest to securing an adoption resembling that of a heterosexual couple. The two were Dr Albert Dykes and the Rev. Jim Dykes, also pastor of a Metropolitan Community Church. They adopted, not a teenage waif, but a two-year-old boy, and did so as an openly homosexual couple wanting to raise a child and willing to consider more adoption in the future. The official single parent was Dr Dykes, a paediatrician, while the Rev. Dykes, who took his partner's surname several years before, was made official guardian.

Some foreign newspapers wrote about the case as if the Dykeses had won a long hard fight. They had not. The adoption was easy. California law permits independent adoptions, without the intervention of an agency, if the natural parent or parents consented. In this case they did. The two new fathers agreed to send the parents a report every year about how the boy – whose name is Robbie – is getting along. Several years later, the Dykeses reported that Robbie was going to nursery school and had settled in nicely. They might adopt another to round out the family.

An easier route to paternity may be in fostering. While there is a shortage of new babies to adopt, because of the Pill and legal abortion, there is no shortage of homeless older children and teenagers. Social agencies are beginning to realize that they should be able to use their skills to detect the elements of a stable foster home among homosexuals willing to offer one. On a London Weekend Television programme on gay life in 1980, a heterosexual teenage boy spoke movingly of the good home he had with his adoptive father and lover. He knows they are gay. He brings his straight friends home. Nobody minds.

While the idea of gay men adopting or fostering children horrifies many otherwise tolerant people, the truth is that the world has long relied on gay men to teach and care for children. With the same exceptions that apply to heterosexuals, they do it well. If people had to apply for a parent licence before having children, who would pass? Gay men should have the same opportunities for surrogate parenthood as any other responsible adult.

11

A Suitable Case for Treatment?

Mr Harding is one of those who never gives his first name. He is an engaging, short, powerfully built young man. A thick blond beard compensates for growing baldness, as does an Addidas T-shirt and crisp new levis. He could be an acrobat but he is a manager for a fast-food shop. He has not resolved his sexual preference and is obviously attractive to women. He has been a reluctant homosexual, trying to become a wholehearted one. It has not been easy. Dr Kinsey would have no difficulty in placing him at 3 or 4, right in the middle of his scale.

'I was twenty-two when I was married. I knew I was gay. And I didn't want to be. I've known I was gay since the age of eight. I had sex with my brother for a couple of years from twelve to fourteen – when *I* was, that is, and he was about three years older. We'd be wrestling in front of the TV and it would end up with sex.

'At the dating stage, I was going out with a girl and going out with a guy at the same time. I read a story about that. I romanticized it. I am not a promiscuous type. With girls, I did a lot of heavy petting, exploring. When I was seventeen, a feller first kissed me. I thought it was disgusting, not the sort of thing a feller should do. Oh yes, a taxi driver followed me onto some waste ground when I was about thirteen and we had anal sex. It was sort of rape. Since then I've always been the active one – put me off it for life, I suppose. I went to the cottages when I was thirteen to fifteen but I sort of cut myself off after that. When I went to night school, I met this guy, an administrator. He played football for the local team. He loved me. I know he loved me. He sent me messages on the backs of Wrigley chewing gum wrappers. 'This is a load of shit,' I thought, and I went out with girls from about eighteen. I had a girl named

142

Sally. I had to tell her that I had previously been with a feller. She was very upset.

'I moved to Bristol. I shared a room with a guy I'd met on a bus, a coloured guy. He was very possessive and I wasn't used to that. Then I went out with this married guy. He had three kids and his wife was very understanding. Then – before I was twenty – I started going out with Mary. I hadn't been to a doctor of any sort before. I went to the local mental hospital. I said I was gay and wanted to be cured. They asked me did I want to be an in-patient or an out-patient. I asked which was the quickest.' (He laughs at himself.) 'I went in-patient because I wanted it over and done with. I had met Mary at work and she appealed very much, small, petite and pretty. We loved each other. And just two months after I came out of hospital, I was arrested in a toilet. For soliciting. I had just been hanging about and this guy I had spoken to was a cop. I got fined. It was traumatic, but I told my girl. "It doesn't matter," she said. "I'll stick by you. You can trust me."

'We weren't sleeping together. She came from a very straight family. I had sex with her just before we were married. We settled down; I had lots of jobs in the retail trade. We bought a house and we had the baby.

'It happened when my wife was away with the child at her parents'. I picked up a man in a toilet and brought him home. I didn't tell him I was married and there were dresses and everything around. I hid the toys, though. But he found out. "You've got half of everything I want," he said, "you've got a little boy." It was a grand passion for about two weeks; I really fell for this guy. He was put off by the fact that I had a wife. He was totally homosexual and was put off by the fact that I had touched a woman.

'I was in bed when my wife came home. "I'm gay," I said. "What does that mean?" she said. I said it was about time she knew what kind of man she'd married. There was heavy trouble for eighteen months. I went to the marriage guidance place and they asked would my wife come in. She said she didn't see why she should: she didn't have any problems, she didn't want to wash her dirty linen in public.

But she made trouble. Every time I was going out, she thought that I was on the razzle. And I wasn't. Our marriage became bad. We were short of money, we'd just bought the house. She was asked by a friend to help out in a pub and there she met this guy . . .'

Was it a relief her having someone else? 'No. It never was. I was so jealous. I used to lie awake in the bedroom when he would drop her off at night. It became a real fight, fists and all that. When I told her about my being gay, I had just wanted her to know me. I was still sleeping with her, all the time. My wife and I have very good sex lives. At times I thought I would like to have another guy in with us, just to watch. One weekend she asked would I like to take the kid out – she had a lack of maternal interest. "My mum can have him," I said, and I took him home. It was a brilliant weekend. When we got back, she was packing; she took the boy, and that was that.

'For my company I went to open up a shop in another town and there was a girl at work who fancied me. I avoided it, I felt guilty. I can't use a woman any more because of my feelings. But this girl was obviously making a play for me. When I knew I was leaving, I sort of . . . succumbed. I couldn't do it at first but then the thought of being transferred relieved me in a way. In my next letter, I'm going to tell her the truth.

'Now I run a shop in Devon. There I met a guy, it's been going on about sixteen months. I only see him weekends. My parents are great. They said they don't care as long as I'm happy.

'My wife will allow me access to the child, but she won't allow my "associates" to see him. She won't allow him to visit me at weekends. I'm taking her to court; it cuts me up. My son and I have a very good relationship. I want one weekend a month and some holidays – I want to take him for Easter. I've asked my mum to ask her.

'I've got a Utopian kind of dream: I'd love to remarry. I was telling some friends last night – I won't use women – but I still feel for women. Fred, my lover, threw a book at me when I said that. It had hurt him. I thought, "Oh

Christ, the same thing's going to happen in reverse." He envies the parent I am. He envies my heterosexuality.'

Can homosexuals shift to heterosexuality? What choices are open to people like Mr Harding who say, 'I know I'm gay and I don't want to be?'

Even to raise the question of treatment will offend many people – there is no more controversial issue within homosexuality today. Some social scientists, as well as the gay liberation movement, are scathing about traditional psychiatry which, as they see it, treats homosexuals expensively for years with the lure of a 'cure' that never materializes and that seeks to eliminate a disease existing only in society's mind, imposing the values of a heterosexual world on someone who offends by being different. Genuine harm can be done to patients, these critics say, by eliminating or dulling their natural source of pleasure and by teaching them to feel self-hatred and guilt. Sometimes (the indictment continues) the therapist does not even tell the patient that a change of sexual preference is what the treatment is aiming at and the objective is pursued by stealth.

Treatment implies disease. Disease implies cure and the duty to seek or to strive for cure. Many ordinary people, as well as those judges who sentence homosexuals to some form of therapy in lieu of prison, believe that homosexuality is like dandruff – a condition that you can get rid of if you will only take the trouble. A woman architect described to the author the advice she gave to a homosexual friend who had been moaning to her about the latest lover he had lost. '"You're not gay," I told him. "You're *queer*! Something's gone terribly *wrong*. Go and get yourself fixed up!"'

Paradoxically, the idea that homosexuality is untreatable is almost equally widespread. It is held by the homosexual movement itself and was fostered by Freud. In his famous letter to an American mother, written in 1935 (in a clear style which his followers unfortunately have been unable to emulate), Freud wrote (in English):

Dear Mrs –
I gather from your letter that your son is a homosexual . . .

145

Homosexuality is assuredly no advantage, but it is nothing to be ashamed of, no vice, no degradation; it cannot be classified as an illness; we consider it to be a variation of the sexual function produced by a certain arrest of sexual development . . .

By asking me if I can help, you mean, I suppose, if I can abolish homosexuality and make normal heterosexuality take its place. The answer is, in a general way we cannot promise to achieve it. In a certain number of cases we succeed in developing the blighted germs of heterosexual tendencies which are present in every homosexual; in the majority of cases it is no more possible. It is a question of the quality and the age of the individual. The result of treatment cannot be predicted.

What analysis can do for your son runs in a different line. If he is unhappy, neurotic, torn by conflicts, inhibited in his social life, analysis may bring him harmony, peace of mind, full efficiency, whether he remains a homosexual or gets changed . . .

Sincerely yours with kind wishes,
Freud

A bleak prognosis wafted also from the British Wolfenden report in 1957: 'We were struck by the fact that none of our medical witnesses were able, when we saw them, to provide any reference in medical literature to a complete change of this kind.' ('Of this kind' meant a 180-degree turn from exclusively homosexual to exclusively heterosexual.)

This sweeping declaration was instrumental in changing English law ten years later so that homosexual acts in private were no longer criminal offences. What cannot be changed must be endured, the Wolfenden reform seemed to say. The argument of incurability, however, does not move everybody. In Ireland in 1980, for example, David Norris, a homosexual, petitioned to have the Irish Acts of 1861 and 1865, making homosexual acts criminal and unconstitutional, struck down. He described himself as 'congenitally, irreversibly and incurably' homosexual and said that 4 per cent of all men in Ireland were the same, not to mention a much larger group with pronounced homosexual tendencies. The court was unmoved; the nineteenth-century laws unchanged.

Congenital? Where does homosexuality come from? The very word 'cause' is taboo to many homosexuals, for it too reeks of disease and cure. The authors of *The Gay Report*, when preparing the questionnaire from whose 5,000 responses their book was based, deliberately refrained from including any questions about family background. 'We felt,' explained Karla Jay and Allen Young, 'that we would turn people off if they felt we were trying to prove, or even disprove, the shrinks' popularized theories of how gay people "get that way".'

Often homosexuals say that the question of cause is meaningless. Why not ask what causes heterosexuality? they ask.

But people do. That is one reason why homosexual protests about the search for causes are ingenuous. The whole study of human personality looks into the origins and the development of sexuality. The difficulty for homosexuals is that most psychological research is based on a theory that they reject – that children go through certain universal stages of emotional progress of which the end result, if there has been no major disturbance, is heterosexuality. The second reason for overruling homosexual protests about causes is that gay men and women spend a lot of time asking themselves how they 'got that way'. Anything that excludes you from a major activity of the human race tends to preoccupy your mind. A deplorable reaction to heterosexual society's prejudice, perhaps – but homosexuals engage in an intense and wide-ranging examination of the possible causes that has to be listened to:

'I think it's nature's way of easing up on overpopulation.'

'It does seem to affect only children and last children. Whatever it is, I'm convinced it's settled by the age of five.'

'I favour a genetic theory rather than the environment. It's like blue-eyedness and brown-eyedness. My cousin is gay.'

A cause need not imply a disease but it does imply a process, a regularly observed sequence of events. Most other human traits are seen in terms of orderly stages of development – intelligence, muscular strength, teeth, sexual organs – why not sexual object-choice? Even this suggestion is repugnant to homosexual apologists. Their goal is to have society treat homosexuality as a conscious preference, like coffee or tea, Labour or Tory, and then to place the same high value on love for the same sex as it places on love of the opposite sex. What they do not see is how their refusal to consider the origins of homosexual behaviour works against their wish for equality. Until the dynamics of sexual preference is better understood, homosexuality will widely be thought to be contagious and homosexuals will be discriminated against in custody cases and applications for jobs dealing with children.

The search for a cause of homosexuality is as old as history. Aristotle and St Thomas Aquinas favoured a biological predisposition. Ancient astrologers believed that certain constellations of the Zodiac produced various sexual tastes, with Venus and Mars especially connected to heterosexuality. As causes, demonic possession and masturbation have had their day. A recent letter to the *Boston Globe* has blamed a diet over rich in dairy food.

During the heyday of psychoanalysis, biological considerations were eclipsed but lately they have shown a new vitality, even though common sense argues against heredity being the dominant cause. Although some homosexuals in any period of history have married, they have tended to do so at a lower rate than do heterosexuals, and to have fewer children. If it were dependent on being passed from father to son, homosexuality would breed itself out.

However, genetic causes have been hard to disprove. The strongest implication that homosexuality is based on an inborn tendency came from research in 1952 on eighty-five pairs of male twins in which at least one of the pair was homosexual. The researcher F. J. Kallman reported that in every one of the forty pairs of identical twins, both brothers had turned out homosexual. Of the other forty-five pairs, all fraternal twins (that is, with dissimilar genes), homosexuality was often found in only one. Did this clinch the argument in favour of heredity once and for all? No. For one thing, none of Kallman's identical twins had been reared apart. Brought up in the same families, living under the same conditions, identical twin brothers could as easily have learned their behaviour as inherited it. For another thing, no subsequent research has been able to duplicate Kallman's findings.

Another possibility being explored is that hormones affecting the foetus before birth may play a part in the development of at least those men with effeminate mannerisms and no heterosexual interest at all. It seems possible that deficiencies of the male hormone during the early months of gestation may predispose the male embryo towards homosexual preference in adult life.

So far, none of the fragmentary research evidence adds up to anything like a cause. The understanding of sexual orientation behaviour is at the stage where that of anatomy was in Leonardo's time. Future research for evidence of an inherited predisposition towards homosexual behaviour will probably look in the direction of prenatal hormonal influences on the brain rather than genes *per se*, but against a background of growing conviction that a predisposition means nothing unless certain circumstances bring homosexuality out.

But what circumstances? Disturbed relations between the young child and his two parents, goes the most widely held theory of the origin of homosexuality. Early home environment, in other words – a short phrase which covers a multitude of warring approaches.

Classical psychoanalysis considers homosexuality to be pathology – an adaptation to hidden but overwhelming fears of the opposite sex. The authoritative analytic view was expressed by Dr Irving Bieber in 1962, that heterosexuality is the biologic norm and that, unless hindered, all individuals are heterosexual. Homosexuals do not bypass heterosexual development but simply stop at an earlier stage. All remain potentially heterosexual. (The name and work of Dr Bieber, along with those of his fellow analyst, Dr Charles Socarides, are treated with scorn by the homosexual movement.) Analysts, said Dr Bieber, should help patients orient themselves to heterosexual objectives, rather than to adjust their homosexual destiny.

To Dr Bieber probably goes the credit, or blame, of originating the 'my mother made me a homosexual' theory. A background frequently found among male homosexuals, he said, was the dominant, over-protecting mother and the cold and rejecting or absent father. The young boy thus grows up with a fear of being swallowed up by the mother, of being literally pulled back into her vagina. In his terror, the boy may even imagine that the vagina has teeth – *vagina dentata*. He then recoils from all women; at the same time he lacks an identification with a strong male, developing a passivity and effeminacy.

Whatever its significance, this combination of parent type is undoubtedly common to many homosexuals. For example, it describes the childhood home of the homosexual playwright, Joe Orton, who was killed by his lover in their Islington flat in 1967. Orton's mother, Elsie, was a big, blowsy, noisy machinist with a collapsed lung; his father, William, was a gardener, frail, cowed, silent. According to Orton's biographer, John Lahr, 'Unwilling and unable to control his family, William never earned its respect. Elsie would scream, "I'm mother and father to this family! I've raised four kids on one lung!" William, constantly mocked by Elsie, never answered back. William was a stranger to his wife, his family and himself. When he was hit by a car and had his skull fractured, his son's comment was "That won't make any difference to his brain".'

There is no denying that many of the male homosexuals interviewed for this book saw their mothers in textbook Bieber terms:

'I've nothing to thank my Dad for. My mother brought us up.'

'I know it's a cliché but I was raised entirely by women. My father died before I was three and I grew up with my mother, my aunt and my sister.'

'My mother wanted me to be a girl. A girl baby before me died at birth. I had two other brothers. She dressed me as a girl until I was three and used to introduce me as her daughter and had me handing around sandwiches at tea parties.'

If he was harsher than Freud in classifying homosexuality as an illness, Bieber also offered more hope. In 1966 he reported that twenty-nine out of 106 homosexual males treated by analysis in New York City had achieved heterosexual shifts, usually after 350 or more hours of analysis.

The weakness in the theory is the millions of obvious exceptions: male homosexuals who have warm, loving fathers and heterosexual sons who have survived devouring mothers and remote fathers. Then too there is the whole of the black society. Long characterized by strong mothers and absent fathers, it does not show any disproportionate gay component. Nor do fatherless families in general. Where they do differ from the ordinary is in problems of all kinds – truancy, poor marks, ill-health. Who is to say whether these result from the absence of the father or of his income? If fatherlessness does produce a tendency towards homosexuality, this can be expressed in heterosexual love-making, masturbation, promiscuity or fantasy, never surfacing in the behaviour marked homosexual. While there probably are family patterns of a more subtle hue that will someday be linked with homosexuality preference, they have not yet been detected and a major Kinsey Institute study backed by the National Institute of Mental Health suggested in 1981 that the parents' role in a child's sexual orientation has been grossly exaggerated and that a deep, possibly biological predisposition is the main factor.

The origins of lesbianism are even more elusive and far less searched for. 'A mother who is not so much demanding as unavailable' is what some analysts suspect. When the girl reaches out for love and for identification, the mother cannot meet her need, either because she is too infantile, self-absorbed or detached. Fathers of lesbians have been seen as overseductive, or passive or cold. Very often lesbians feel that they are lacking in femininity. Some also have a loathing of heterosexual intercourse – a parallel to the male dread of the vagina. As feminists might observe, however, real vaginas do not have teeth; women can have intercourse against their will. Many more women who describe themselves as exclusively lesbian have had heterosexual intercourse in their lifetimes than have Kinsey 5 or Kinsey 6 men.

Bolstered by feminism, lesbians make an even louder claim than do male homosexuals to embody a choice, not an abnormality. The American poetess, Adrienne Rich, for example, widow, mother of three sons, chose lesbianism in mid-life. She wanted to live in a world of women as a protest against the male-centred society that has enforced and institutionalized 'seemingly natural states of being, like heterosexuality, like motherhood' to deprive women of their power. She asks that interviewers mention her lesbianism.

If there is any common ground in current psychiatric thinking, it is that homosexual erotic preference is the result of experiences during the very early years, certainly before six or seven, acting upon people who perhaps may be vulnerable through genetic inheritance. It does not have one cause, but many. It quite frequently appears in later life, among people who suddenly give up a heterosexual life. Some element of chance is involved – meeting just the right man or woman – but such people frequently have had an active homosexual life in fantasy for many years.

Research does seem to have disproved one part of analytic theory – that homosexuality is part of a parcel of neurotic symptoms, the sign of a 'sick' person. The work of Dr Evelyn Hooker and more recently the Kinsey Institute has revealed that homosexuals by and large are psychologically normal, distinguished from heterosexuals only by their choice of erotic object. Homosexuality, as Dr Hooker defined it, is a variant in sexual patterning within the normal psychological range.

In 1973 the American Psychiatric Association was won over. It voted to remove homosexuality from its diagnostic manual of mental disorders. Homosexuality in itself, declared the APA, implies no impairment in judgement, stability or reliability. The association called for an end to discrimination against homosexuals.

Was the APA resolution a great advance for homosexual equality, or a sell-out to a pressure group? The battle still rages. Both sides may be right. Conference resolutions cannot eliminate prejudice, but they can steer public opinion and encourage the faint-hearted. Following the APA's lead, conservative organizations such as the American Bar Association and the American Medical Association called for an end to state laws making private adult homosexual acts criminal. The American Federation of Teachers and the US Civil Service Commission, as described in chapter 7, asked for homosexuality to be dropped as a barrier to employment.

Yet if homosexuality were no longer officially illness, was it correspondingly declared health? What about its treatment by psychiatry? Since 1974 there has been a strong backlash from the psychiatric profession against the APA's action, which had been in effect the decision of a small committee. In its understandable desire to eliminate discrimination against a minority, the critics said, the APA had substituted political for scientific judgement. The much-publicized resolution had de-intellectualized psychiatry, putting three-quarters of a century's accumulated knowledge about how the personality grows and about the importance of the libido into the realm of opinion, where one view is as good as any other.

In the *American Journal of Psychiatry* in 1977, Edward Levine and Nathaniel Ross (respectively a sociologist and a psychoanalyst) argued that admirable humanistic ideals did not require homosexuality to be regarded as a natural sexual expression. The danger, in their view, was that parents may come to consider homosexuality as natural as heterosexuality in their children, instead of a sign of a disturbed emotional development. The opportunities to help children at what therapists consider an amenable age – well before puberty – to resolve a developing social conflict may be lost. And if heterosexuality is no longer considered a basic cultural value, attention to the art of being a good parent, particularly at the child's oedipal stage, may be neglected.

In individual lives, however, the theoretical question is irrelevant. What most people want to know is whether a choice exists. If there is a fork in the road of sexual

153

orientation, where does it appear – in early childhood, in adolescence, at any point in life? What about sexually uncertain young people? Must they accept any homosexual feeling as a sign of their true orientation and try to learn to be glad to be gay? Can they shift themselves towards heterosexuality if they decide they are equally poised between the two?

The answer is that some can change – if they want to. The 'choice', if it can be properly called that, occurs as early as six or seven. What can happen later is a reversal of choice or a resolution of confusion. It helps if those seeking change are young, if they have some heterosexual tendencies already and if they can accept the likelihood that they will never be totally free from arousal by their own sex. To gay people these qualifications add up to a description of a suppressed homosexual, not a 'changed one', like the reformed alcoholic, or the left-hander who has been forced to write with the right hand. Anybody can give up anything – that is not news.

Therapists of various persuasions, however, claim more than suppression. If homosexual preference is learned behaviour, their reasoning goes, it should respond to stimuli to learning. These stimuli can be a transference relationship with a therapist; they can be mechanical aids, like drugs, or electric shock, or they can be the deliberate rituals and peer pressure used in the combination of behavioural techniques and group therapy. In shifting homosexual preference, therapists do not see the obstacle lying in the potent magic or ease of making love to a person of the same sex, contrary to what many people believe. They see it in the difficulty of giving up any source of familiar gratification.

In 1972, before the American Psychiatric Association had sanitized homosexuality, the National Institute of Mental Health published a major report on the subject. The report is still valuable because of its cautious summary of the prognosis for homosexuals in various forms of treatment. Since then the results have improved. The NIMH found that of homosexuals desiring treatment, somewhere

154

between 10 and 20 per cent of those exclusively homosexual could be helped to shift towards a heterosexual adjustment. Of bisexuals – those in mid-Kinsey scale, the dominant group presenting itself for treatment – up to 40 per cent could become essentially heterosexual. (To put it another way, most will fail.)

The evidence upon which the NIMH drew this conclusion was pitifully scant and based on two fuzzy definitions of 'success', lenient and stringent. 'Lenient' meant any detectable shift at all; 'stringent' meant that the patient enjoyed and could perform heterosexually with little residual homosexual interest. The NIMH assessed three forms of treatment: psychoanalysis, group therapy, and aversion therapy involving the use of electric shock or a drug to induce vomiting. All related to males. Few lesbians (as later researchers have confirmed) present themselves for treatment relating to their sexual preference.

All of the treatments helped highly motivated homosexuals to some degree, the NIMH learned, and there was no way to decide among them. Patients sent by the courts did poorly; so did those on the rebound from a broken homosexual love affair.

Two aversion techniques were studied. In one, the patient was given a drug to make him vomit when shown male pin-ups. In another, looking at the same kind of photographs, he was punished with an electric shock immediately followed by a picture of a female nude as a form of relief. An Orwellian nightmare? To the cold eye of the NIMH, aversion therapies looked just as successful as the 'talking cures' – or more so, considering how much less time and money they took.

Needless to say, the homosexual movement finds these aversion therapies the most offensive of all. Many psychiatrists in the 1980s have given up using them because they are embarrassingly crude and ineffective. The case for the opposition was best put by the poet, W. H. Auden: 'Of course, Behaviourism "works", so does torture.'

The analysts claimed the greatest percentages of improvement, but their standards for diagnosis and outcome were highly subjective and inconsistent. (Two of the analysts followed procedures which are now common under the wing of sex therapy – giving their patient instructions in detail on how to make a date and how to have sexual intercourse. One of these analysts, Dr Lawrence Hatterer, has described his technique in his book with the frank title, *Changing Homosexuality in the Male*. He tries to train homosexuals to notice the kinds of situation which lead them to seek out anonymous orgasms in public places – feelings of depression, perhaps, or loneliness, much the same as propel an alcoholic towards a drink, or an addict towards a fix. Hatterer's approach in general is to praise heterosexuality and boost confidence without denigrating homosexuality: not 'stop it', but 'try it'.)

Any of these procedures for treating homosexuality stresses the importance of motivation. 'It is desirable,' concluded the NIMH, 'to combat the sense of hopelessness and inevitability so prevalent among homosexuals by widely publicizing the fact that current treatment methods enable about one-fifth of exclusive homosexuals to achieve some heterosexual interest and competence if they really wish to do so and that a much higher percentage of persons with some heterosexual orientation can be helped to become predominantly heterosexual.'

The intimations that many homosexuals can be helped to have a heterosexual life, with occasional lapses, however, mean that a great many people are expected to accept the strains of living with a spouse struggling against homosexuality. The NIMH report called for more study of the effects on families of living with a homosexual member, but it ignored the special problems of the spouse.

In more recent years, new behavioural therapies have come into prominence, claiming very high success rates of converting homosexuals to heterosexuality. The most influential results have been claimed by the Masters and Johnson rapid form of therapy for sexual malfunction. Their claim to have altered homosexual preferences in 75 per cent of the cases reported in their *Homosexuality in Perspective* has been

156

admired and also ridiculed. Masters and Johnson, it has been said, are so careful to screen out unlikely failures in advance that their results are bound to be good. They have also been criticized for treating only couples – an alleged sign of prejudice in favour of monogamy and close relationships. Nonetheless, Masters and Johnson have pioneered techniques at their institute at St Louis which have encouraged a new profession of sex therapists, and helped thousands of people for whom sexual problems are a particular source of unhappiness.

As part of their work, Masters and Johnson found that they had become perhaps the first to try to treat the homosexual for poor performance. Every one of the homosexuals who came to them for ordinary sexual complaints, such as premature ejaculation or impotence, had been rejected when seeking professional help. While these disabilities are as much a misery when the lover is of the same as of the opposite sex, the medical and psychiatric professions seem to have considered a malfunctioning homosexual to be either a contradiction in terms or beyond help.

Along with those homosexuals who wanted to be more effective as homosexuals, Masters and Johnson took into treatment a group of sixty-seven men and women who presented themselves as 'dissatisfied' homosexuals – gay, and not wanting to be. Either to shift to heterosexuality or revert to it was their wish. Nearly two-thirds were married men. Some had left their wives and were living as homosexuals; the rest were still at home, either sexually withdrawn from their wives or leading double lives, sleeping with the wife and with lovers as well. Three of the seven married lesbians were active as lesbians with their husbands' knowledge. Two others had husbands who were not aware of the lesbianism until their wives told them they wanted to enter sex-preference therapy, and needed the husbands to join them. People coming only to please a spouse were rejected on grounds of low motivation, as were those who wanted to get a better job, or who wanted to become '95 per cent' heterosexual. Masters and Johnson, who insist that they are genuinely neutral towards their patients' sexual preferences, nonetheless would not collaborate in helping homosexual men mislead their wives, pretending to seek a cure when they were not.

The treatment techniques are the same for hetero- or homosexual couples. They require a pair of therapists, one man and one woman. The patient has to bring a partner or a willing friend. (Masters and Johnson used to use paid 'surrogates' to work with single patients, but abandoned them. Any friend who volunteers for the course has to be prepared to co-operate for a few months afterwards, on the theory that sexual intercourse is like driving or swimming. Especially if you have had to overcome fear to learn how to do it, you have to keep on doing it once you've mastered it or otherwise you'll lose the knack.) The couple then goes through a thorough physical examination and individually gets instruction in the anatomy and physiology of the sexual response of the opposite sex. What follows then is instruction in 'non-genital' touching and massage. The sex organs are declared out of bounds; the sensual possibilities of the other parts are then to be explored. The couple is urged to adopt code words so that they can communicate during sex without a lot of verbiage. When one partner feels anxious, he or she must say the code word, whereupon the other is to forget about trying to please and concentrate on personal satisfaction. Nothing is a greater passion-killer, according to the Masters and Johnson school, than monitoring one's own performance.

The treatment is concentrated into fourteen days. The love exercises are performed in private, as homework. Contrary to popular belief, the therapist team does not watch. (Researchers have watched couples in action as part of the Masters and Johnson studies of sexual response, however.) Although the literary style of Masters and Johnson is guaranteed to ward off thrill-seekers ('admittedly a penetrative act, fellatio creates only minor nomenclature confusion because the male does not need even a partial erection for oral penetration'), in its own way, their work makes romantic reading. There is, for example, the story of the Kinsey 6 man who falls in love with a Kinsey 0 woman and learns to consummate an unconsummated marriage.

Another tale tells of the marriage in which the main problem was not the husband's homosexual experiences, but the wife's rigid Roman Catholicism, reinforced by obstetrical troubles. What the priest did not forbid, the gynaecologist ruled out. No variations on the conventional positions of love making, no intercourse during pregnancy. During therapy, however, it was the wife who changed first. She proved an apt and inventive pupil and convinced her husband that he wanted his marriage as a way of life. As their mutual pleasure in sex increased, so did their ordinary communication and so did the state of their marriage, and 'his homosexual orientation was neutralized by his own choice'.

Another man who was divorced by his wife for sexual incompetence had a long relationship with a male lover until rumours started that threatened his career. The lover encouraged him to begin dating women. Then (too good to be true?) he met a widow, older and well-off, who agreed to help him try to regain his lost heterosexuality. Together they went to the Masters and Johnson Institute, which rated him Kinsey 4. With therapy, his heterosexual competence returned; he was 'inordinately pleased'. Told that the choice of sexual preference was his alone to decide, he unhesitatingly chose heterosexuality.

There was a Kinsey 6 woman, thirty-one years old, a lesbian for eleven years, who had decided that homosexuality had little to offer and had gone out, found herself a man she wanted to marry, and entered therapy. She was the only child of a dull marriage, with a disciplinarian mother and a permissive father. She was introduced to homosexual caressing by an aunt, with whom she later went to live. The aunt and all her friends were lesbian; the girl performed sexual acts with them. But she had never had an orgasm, even from masturbation. When men approached, she withdrew.

At the age of thirty, when she met a man she was attracted to, she blamed her sexual fears on her virginity. Time and again, however, they could not consummate the sex act. Finally, she told him about her lesbian past and asked him to join her in treatment. He agreed, declaring that he wanted to marry her even if the treatment were unsuccessful.

Prospects were pretty poor – the woman suffered both from vaginismus (involuntary vaginal spasms) and from fear of semen. The spasms were treated by the Masters and Johnson technique of inserting plastic dilators in graduated sizes (by the girl and then her lover) until the spasms had stopped. After ten days of therapy, she had her first orgasm and was frightened when she did not know what it was. She was in tears 'when later reassured that she had simply experienced the birthright of sexual expression'. The couple eventually married and had a child. The wife did not report any resurgence of interest in homosexual activity.

The reported success results of these treatments are high, even if expressed, as Masters and Johnson modestly did, in terms of a failure rate of 25 per cent. Of the dissatisfied males and female homosexuals in sum, nearly three-quarters achieved their goal of heterosexual orientation. The men did slightly better than the women but not by very much.

However, the success rate was far higher for the homosexuals who wanted to become better at homosexuality – 90 per cent. These people were also far more co-operative as patients and research participants. They reported back for follow-up reports and tended to stay in the same place. The 'changed' homosexuals, in contrast, were disinclined to be re-interviewed, and often could not be relocated. Perhaps, Masters and Johnson conjectured, they did not want to be reminded of their homosexual past, especially if they had made new relationships without confiding the details of their past to their new partners. Perhaps – something Masters and Johnson did not suggest – they had reverted to homosexuality.

Equal, if not better results have been obtained from a combination of behavioural techniques and weekly group psychotherapy. Dr Lee Birk of Harvard Medical School and Learning Therapies Inc., has claimed to have achieved reversal of preference in fourteen out of fourteen cases in one group. Birk, like many therapists, observes how very few homosexual women, in contrast to homosexual men, seek psychiatric treatment for their sexual preference in itself. He and his wife, also a therapist, have a good rapport with the gay community and in his published work he meets the opposition head on by stating his views:

There is no monolithic disease called 'homosexuality'. The right of an individual to choose a homosexual or bisexual adaptation should be adequately protected by law and custom. However, for men who are homosexual or bisexual and who are not happy with this adaptation, or who are in general unhappy, psychotherapy by male-female group therapy can be a highly effectual and efficient treatment low in cost. The shifts achieved are not total metamorphoses of the personality. Most who have been homosexual continue to have some homosexual interest. Most continue to have some homosexual encounters even while being what they consider happily married.

The heart of the Birk therapy is the man-woman team of therapists, working with homosexuals in groups. The team provides each member of the group with a live, built-in oedipal triangle. As most of the men have felt too close to their mothers and too distant from their fathers and unable to relate to both parents at the same time, they vent these feelings left over from childhood against the therapists. If the patients persevere, they learn to differentiate between their past and present feelings and try out new ones, especially affection for the woman. At first, homosexual members of the group, Birk observed, often take pains to drive a wedge between the gays, themselves, and the straight therapists. They try to shock with tales of Turkish baths and lavatory blow-jobs. Yet as the sessions progress, they also help each other, putting pressure on each other to give up effeminate behaviour or to explain why they went on cruising. They mocked a man who was going to accept, as a wedding present from his mother, a make of car he didn't want. What the therapists concentrate on are the personal side of sexual relations, the artificiality of

161

dividing people into gay and straight, and the neurotic ingredients shown in the patients' sexual behaviour of any kind. (Success can spur anonymous sex as much as anger or failure; one of the patients went straight to a subway lavatory after being praised in public by his law professor.)

Some of Birk's results have been no less than spectacular. Out of his group of fourteen highly motivated, exclusively homosexual patients, who wanted to shift, all were able to experience sex with a woman after about two and a half years of weekly therapy. Ten out of fourteen married and remained married. In another group, of homosexuals who did not seek a change of orientation as their major objective, only one achieved it. These results might allay homosexuals' fears about 'being changed against their will'.

Such figures, however, will not allay any fears about women being sucked into unrewarding or difficult marriages without understanding or realizing it. For example, Birk and associates report the case of John, an only child, a strict Catholic, an altar boy, seduced by a priest. John came into therapy with a sex history of occasional sex contacts with young boys, much masturbation to boys' photographs and no experience or fantasy with females. During the course of group therapy, he got married to a quiet Catholic girl. The honeymoon was what you would expect – painfully disappointing. He and his wife Judy began direct sex therapy. After four months of weekly sessions, they managed intercourse. Consummation, however, 'while a real therapeutic landmark on its own, did not mark the beginning of a problem-free sexual union'. Indeed it did not. Unknown to Judy, John began a sexual relationship with a young boy named Terry. Remaining within the group therapy (which his wife did not attend), John realized the complicated longings for a father and a son that lay behind his attraction to Terry. The marital sex improved. Finally he was able to tell Terry that the sexual side of their relationship would stop although their friendship would continue. 'About six weeks later, with deliberate casualness, John announced in group that he and Judy were expecting a baby in the spring.'

162

Success? What about Judy? Should not she have been told of the threat to her marriage that existed before she undertook her pregnancy?

Many homosexuals and many analysts for different reasons argue that a shift should never be attempted. One Hampstead analyst who specializes in sexual problems summarized his approach: 'Many a homosexual has come in here saying, "I want treatment but don't you dare touch my homosexuality!" I never encourage them to do anything. With analysis, they can become happier homosexuals. There are a lot of different kinds of homosexuality observed in analytic practice. Some are more amenable to treatment than others. There is the man who is a latent heterosexual, who really wants to be heterosexual. If it is fear of women or fear of the sexual act that prevents it, that fear may well respond to analysis. The deeper kind has a lot of paranoia involved. It is not the homosexuality in itself, but the use they make of it. It can be a protection against deep depression – in that sense, gay is a good word. Then there are the narcissists, looking for their own beauty. They want to be adored, their true self to be valued. The love of an older man for a beautiful boy, as in *Death in Venice*, is pathological because the means taken ensure that it is doomed to failure.

'The search for the father is very important – the younger boy looking for the older man – but that in itself is linked to flight from the mother. The common type of homosexual who is living happily at home with his mother is in fact terrified of getting too close to her. He has to withdraw from her, by avoiding all women.

'In general, I have no doubt that homosexuality is pathology. I don't think that the happy settled homosexual couple can relate to each other the way a happily married heterosexual couple can, although I have a homosexual friend, who has been with a lover five years now, who I know would disagree with me. The homosexual act can contain more infantile and sado-masochistic elements than heterosexual intercourse. Heterosexual love allows for the real fulfilment of infantile needs. Some forms, of course, are equally doomed – the older man with his young girlfriend. Yet I don't like the idea that homosexuality is a development that somehow has stopped a stage early on the road to heterosexuality. I think we have learned more about it since Freud. I prefer to think that it is an early shift to a different line of development.

'From my practice, I think I can say that homosexuals use the psychological defence of splitting more than heterosexuals do. The married man who loves his wife but goes to the cottages is a classic example of splitting. He maintains his love for his wife by excluding the whole range of himself from her. When he sticks his penis through a hole in the public toilet wall, he is in no danger of being emotionally involved. In his moment of ultimate abandonment, he is alone.

'One of my patients was a schoolmaster, a very caring person who specialized in the most difficult pupils. The ones that no one else could do anything with, they gave to him. He was proud of that. Yet he once picked up a sixteen year old boy and seduced him. The cry of pain the boy gave when he penetrated him is what gave him his greatest pleasure. My job as an analyst is to point out the separation of feelings – the kindness, gentleness and pride in himself as a teacher from the pleasure in causing pain.

'I know that homosexuals say they have a great advantage in lovemaking because they understand exactly what the other person is feeling. But that seems masturbatory. If the other person is like one's self, one is in effect doing it with one's self. It's the not knowing, the *vive la différence*, that takes it beyond mutual masturbation and into an adventure and sharing.

'Yes, I believe there is a choice. Homosexuals can change. Adolescence is when the choices are made, no matter what early experience has been. Fancying one's own sex is not necessarily a worrying symptom – if it has been restricted to fantasy. If one's body has actually experienced it, it is harder to get over, to reverse it – if that is what one wants.'

Homosexuals seeking psychiatric help of any kind should

take great care in choosing their psychiatrist. If they want one from the psychiatric mainstream who is gay, they can find one. Each will spell out a personal view of the determinants of homosexuality if asked. 'We ought to regard sexual orientation as "innate",' one gay psychiatrist ventured, 'that is, if not genetic, at least a very deeply structured part of one's personality which isn't like a neurotic symptom that can be ironed out through therapy. Traditional psychiatrists see conflict, but I can only say that I think the march of evidence will prove them wrong.'

Several of the homosexuals interviewed for this book paid tributes to psychiatry, not only for helping them to live with their homosexuality but for revealing it to them.

A Jewish refugee who came to London during the war recalls how she took an overdose of pills and crawled into the bushes at Hyde Park. Attempted suicide at that time in Britain was an indictable offence. The police who pulled her out told her that if she sought psychiatric help, she would not be prosecuted. She went to the Tavistock Institute and told them her problem, which included the fact that sexual intercourse made her nauseated. A kindly woman analyst told her she was 'decidedly homosexual'. 'The word "lesbian" terrified me,' she remembers. 'But she explained about the androgyny in us all. At first I tried sleeping around to prove that she was wrong but soon I met a woman – it was like coming home. Emotionally, I was together at last. "You're not weird," I told myself. "This is life again."' She has always been grateful to the psychiatrist and always wondered whether the analyst were lesbian herself.

An art professor recalls how, as a young married man, he went to the Menninger Clinic in Kansas, asking for a 'complete change'. The psychiatrist he got, he now thinks back with wry gratitude, saved his sanity. 'He led me rapidly through a redefining and accepting of the sexual condition, of my beingness – what I am. (He was so handsome I nearly went out of my mind.) I accepted being gay, got divorced. Today, as a result, my philosophy is, "If

I am a cocksucker, I will be the best there is. It is a beautiful, wonderful thing, an act of joy."'

How far have these therapies actually travelled from the kindly family doctor or priest or minister advising the uncertain young man to find himself a nice girl and settle down? In a more subtle way it looks as if marriage is still being pushed as a cure. The new breed of therapists offer hope of 'change' for those who are gay and don't want to be if they have strong motivation. What better sign of motive than marriage or commitment to a heterosexual partner? What better reward for the idealized parent that the therapist becomes than to announce an engagement or a pregnancy? And for the majority of sexually confused young people who will never go near a psychiatrist, marriage will still look like a worthwhile gesture of intent: 'This is the direction I want to follow'.

For the new therapist, marriage is still the badge of success. They may be creating a demand for a new generation of latter-day saints, spouses who must be understanding and sympathetic, without ever slipping into the detachment of sex therapists.

There is one remaining tactic for change from gay to straight that has to be considered: marriage itself. For all those who marry in the false hope of shifting them away from homosexuality, there must be a certain number for whom the experience of marriage works. Theirs are the true unrecorded voices. If there is a genuine continuum of sexuality, then there must be millions of people sliding into heterosexuality for all those who slide the other way. Some must grow out of it.

A ribald account of a long journey into straightness is told by the jazz musician, George Melly, in his autobiographies. In *Rum, Bum and Concertina*, he portrays his youth as one of the buggery champions of the Royal Navy. One afternoon in a London flat above Brook Street he was initiated into the other kind of sex by a married woman friend, who, with her husband, disapproved of 'my total commitment to arse'. Melly knew, from conversations with his shipmates, what to do, although he did perform with hidden amusement. Gradually, in his other volume, *Owning Up*, he becomes converted to the idea that 'girls like it too' and shifts over. With equal enthusiasm at the end of his story, he portrays himself as a happily married man with children. Does he miss the past? 'Some ask', he says, and 'more think.' His answer:

> No. I read a book recently by a man now dead called Verrier Elwin. He was a marvellous old man who spent most of his life in India. He wrote this: Today, and for many years past, my old loves have been concentrated on my beloved wife, in whom I have found the essence of them all. I am a better lover for those experiences.

12

Remedy against Sin

First it was ordained for the procreation of children, to be
brought up in the fear and nurture of the Lord and to the praise
of his Holy Name.
Secondly, it was ordained for a remedy against sin, and to avoid
fornication; that such persons as have not the gift of continency
might marry and keep themselves undefiled members of Christ's
body.
Thirdly, it was ordained for the mutual society, help and
comfort, that the one ought to have of the other, both in
prosperity and adversity.

Book of Common Prayer
On the purpose of marriage, 1662

Homosexuality poses much tougher questions for religion
than for law. Legally, homosexual acts are either offences
under certain conditions or they are not. Religion concerns
itself with private behaviour, with hearts and minds. Not
only what you do but what you think you are doing matters.
The new recognition of the number of homosexuals and the
justice of their demands for equal rights has put the formal
religions into a dilemma from which there is no visible exit,
for it has come as part of their new respect for the
importance of sexuality in every human life.

Did the Creator really mean to exclude 4 per cent of
mankind from love and marriage? Is marriage the only way
that God wants sexual love expressed? If all love comes
from God, can a church compromise on two classes of
human love – one blessed, the other tolerated?

The problem is cruellest for the Protestant churches.
Under Pope John Paul II, the Roman Catholic Church has
not budged from the 1975 Vatican Declaration on Sexual
Ethics that homosexual acts are intrinsically disordered – a
rigid stand that, followed by a recommendation for understanding, leaves priests room for considerable sympathy in

168

the confessional. The Muslim view has been well illustrated by recent execution of homosexuals. Jewish religious groups have managed to steer clear of formal controversy on the issue (although the pressure on any Jewish boy to take a Jewish wife and propagate the race is still formidable). But the Protestants have to carry the burden of their flexibility and diversity. New understanding of sexual behaviour requires new responses and apart from the extreme liberal left wing, the Protestant churches, in spite of numerous working parties and study commissions, are not finding it easy.

Not that outright condemnation relieves even the Catholic Church from wrestling with the meaning of homosexuality. Its theologians, who tend to be Freudians these days, see homosexuality as a developmental adaptation, which consequently raises questions about the morality of a homosexual who does not seek a cure. Yet there are tougher and more interesting theological puzzles, going back to the days of St Augustine, St Bonaventure and St Jerome. If a married person engages in a homosexual act, is it adultery? This ancient puzzle continues to be debated within the Sacred Roman Rota and the regional tribunals as Catholics petition, with increasing frequency, for annulments of marriage.

The answer, with reservations, is no. Homosexual acts, by scholastic reasoning, do not result in 'the perfect division of the flesh' – a canonical legal term for the damage done by adultery to the bond of marriage which makes husband and wife one flesh. The reason is that homosexual acts cannot result in the procreation of children, and therefore are not in themselves a break in the marriage promise to give the spouse an exclusive right to one's body. However, there is a minority view which has been steadily heard down through the centuries and which holds that copulation with the same sex is as destructive to the marriage bond as copulation with the opposite sex. The conflict between the two views may still be debated in deciding upon an individual case.

The fact is that in canon law, homosexuality in itself does

169

not constitute a ground for annulment. Annulments are granted only on certain traditional grounds: an intention not to have children; impotence; an inner reservation that the marriage bond is dissoluble; lack of a clear understanding of the solemnity of marriage (a good all-purpose clause) and an inner determination to violate the marriage through adultery.

There has been a big surge in annulments in recent years, thanks to more generous interpretations of the grounds, particularly of what constitutes a full and reasoned act of consent to entering the permanent and binding state of marriage. In many of these – as many as one-third of the annulments granted in one area, according to an estimate – homosexuality, in one or other partner, is the underlying cause. But homosexuality is not an absolute bar, a 'diriment impediment', to marriage in the way that close degrees of kinship are. A wife who discovered that her husband had married her in the hope of curing his homosexuality would not be any surer of gaining Church-approved freedom than did the Italian countess whose case in 1929 is part of the annals of canon law.

Before she was twenty, Countess Doria married a Count Norbett. They were happy at first and had a child. Then she learned that he was an active homosexual and got a civil divorce. However, she wanted an annulment from the Church. She claimed that her marriage was invalid on three grounds: (1) that the count had not intended to enter into a permanent marriage; (2) that he had in advance determined to continue his homosexuality; and (3) that he lacked free will and had been led by fate to marry. She lost and appealed; the case was heard by a second round of judges. The count himself even appeared to testify to help her out. To no avail. The Rota judges decided that it was not proved that Count Norbett had formed an intention before the marriage to continue his homosexual life. In fact, they observed, he had married precisely to cure his unnatural tendencies. There was no annulment and the marriage – at least in the light of the Church and eternity – remained intact.

The nicety of the distinctions that annulment cases require celibate theologians to make is dazzling. Is it permissible to use homosexual fantasies to enable one to perform one's conjugal duties? (Yes.) Women have always presented theological problems, and easily inflamed feminists should keep away from the texts of the sacred Roman Rota. In the sixteenth and seventeenth centuries, the attempt to apply rules formed in terms of male sexual organs for female homosexuality raised the same question that later troubled Queen Victoria's ministers: were women capable of penetrating each other and therefore of committing 'sodomy'? The solution adopted, according to William Tobin's excellent book, *Homosexuality and Marriage*, was that if one of the women had a clitoris sufficiently large to penetrate the other, a consummated or perfect sodomitic act had taken place. And how, another question arose in annulment cases, can 'psychic impotence' be proved in women, 'whose sole function in intercourse is not to impede male penetration'? To find a female equivalent of the emission of seed – semen – in sodomitic acts, it was decided to consider the vulvovaginal secretions as seed.

The rank of homosexual acts in the hierarchy of sins ought to have been settled by St Thomas Aquinas. In his *Summa Theologica* he declared that sins contrary to nature were morally more base than adultery or fornication. Yet these acts often do not feel that way to those who perform them. Homosexual husbands, for example, became indignant when asked by the author if they considered themselves to be adulterers:

'I have never looked at another woman. I just couldn't do that to my wife.'

'That would be cheating. That wouldn't be fair.'

'I have always been faithful to my wife' (a man who had had several hundred homosexual partners).

The tones of absolute shock, horror and revulsion with which husbands say that they would never do *that* reveals, in an almost Freudian sense, that these men regard homosexual sex, like masturbation, as less important for it does not carry the same commitment to someone else or the threat to their marriage as would extramarital intercourse with another woman.

This belief about the lower ranking of homosexual sin is hardly new. In France in the fourteenth century, the villagers of Montaillou in the Pyrenees were hauled in for a rigorous inquisition by a zealous local bishop (who later became Pope Benedict XII). What they did and thought about sex was written down and recently reproduced in Emmanuel Le Roy Ladurie's book *Montaillou*.

A member of the order of Minorites, Arnaud de Verniolles, confessed how he was initiated into sodomy by his schoolmaster, with whom he shared a bed. A bizarre accident confirmed his homosexuality – or so he told his inquisitors:

> At the time when they were burning the lepers, I was living in Toulouse; one day I "did it" with a prostitute. And after I had perpetrated this sin, my face began to swell. I was terrified and thought I had caught leprosy; I thereupon swore that in future I would never sleep with a woman again; in order to keep this oath, I began to abuse little boys.
>
> I even thought, in the simplicity of my heart, that sodomy and ordinary fornication were indeed mortal sins, but much less serious than the deflowering of virgins, adultery or incest.

Many of today's closet Christian homosexuals would agree that oral sex is less sinful than anal sex and that receiving it is somehow less worrying than administering it. Indeed, the ability of some adolescent males (or guardsmen) to accept money for allowing fellatio to be performed upon them, without thinking of themselves as either prostitutes or homosexuals, is well documented. Moreover, as Laud Humphreys's *Tearoom Trade* revealed, for the strict Catholic, oral homosexual sex may even seem a lesser sin than practising contraception.

Of the married men whom Humphreys had secretly observed having oral sex in public toilets, 63 per cent turned out to be partners in marriages in which at least one person was Roman Catholic. The marriages showed the same pattern: conjugal relations becoming rare after the birth of the last child. There was also a disproportionately high showing of Episcopalians.

Humphreys's conclusion (echoing the Masters and Johnson case quoted earlier) was that the religious teachings to which most of these families adhered may have been the cause of the husbands seeking sex in the tearooms. Many of the men turned to the tearooms after their wives said they did not want more children, and had objected to using artificial birth control. By seeking impersonal sex, they thought they were preserving their marriages, not destroying them. Humphreys found no evidence that the men wanted homosexual contact as such, even less than they wanted the emotional drama and expense of a love affair with a woman. 'They want,' he concluded 'a form of orgasm-producing activity that is less lonely than masturbation and less involving than a love relationship.'

With so little committed, how could they have a burning sense of sin? The same question might be applied to those who have done the opposite and concentrated their love in a single homosexual relationship. A lesbian, brought up as a Catholic, married and separated, living permanently with the woman she never wants to leave, has neither much guilt, nor any wish to get a divorce from the man she has not seen for fourteen years. She explained her philosophy: 'Is it a sin to be a lesbian? No. I don't think so. The number of the sexes was not absolutely equal so heterosexuality was unworkable from the beginning. Clearly, it bothers me. I go to confession, on and off. I tend to try to go where there's a complete stranger. You select out what you say, don't you? You think you've said the lot but you haven't. Homosexuality's supposed to be wrong but I don't think it's wrong and I can't stop it. That's all you have to say, isn't it? Basically the priests say "Well . . . try." Basically, that's what the Pope said. I've never found priests unwilling to accept it. I can't make myself feel all that sorry. The Catholics have centuries of experience behind them. I've always found them less rabid and more forgiving than all the others. My friend and I are both firmly convinced Christians. My marriage doesn't exist and hasn't for

173

twenty-odd years. I couldn't go to a Protestant church. That would be totally wrong.'

Since Pope John Paul II, the 'be it, but don't do it' philosophy has been made more explicit, but even in Catholic Italy, homosexuals are forcing the Church to face the meaning of its total ban on any kind of homosexual act. A young homosexual from Turin wrote to *La Stampa*: 'Ignorant sinner that I am and unwilling to disobey the Church, since it condemns homosexuality so drastically, without any distinction whatsoever, without offering any alternative except to deprive a human being of his own sexual life, nothing remains for me but to hope in the mercy of God.' In America the gay Catholic organization, Dignity, expresses the wish of thousands of Americans to be both homosexual and Catholic.

Protestant churches find it awkward to lay down such a hard line. For them the first big hurdle is the question of the acceptability of homosexual love; then they face the problem of ordination. In 1979 twenty-three bishops of the Episcopal Church at their conference of bishops in Denver, Colorado, issued a statement of conscience explaining why they were in favour of the ordination of homosexuals, when the conference as a whole had resolved against their ordination. In taking a bold stand, the minority had wanted to pay tribute to the part that homosexual clergy have played for years in the work of the church. Yet they had to weave a careful verbal tightrope to explain why they thought homosexual sex is not sinful:

> Not all of these persons [gay clergymen] have necessarily been celibate; and in the relationships of many of them, maintained in the face of social hostility and against great odds, we have seen a redeeming quality which in its way and according to its mode is no less a sign to the world of God's love than is the more usual sign of Christian marriage. From such relationships we cannot believe God to be absent.

That belief in itself raises the question about the concept of split levels of love – heterosexual (God present) and homosexual (God not absent). Having gone thus far, the dissenting bishops were immediately faced with the stickier question of the promiscuity of male homosexuals. Is that God's love too?

With Christian charity, in their statement of conscience, the bishops seemed to gulp and say 'yes – in a way'. They acknowledged the existence of others, who, 'wrestling responsibly with the Christian implications of their sexuality seek to be responsible . . . even in the occasionally more transient relationships which the hostility of our society towards homosexual persons – with its concomitants of furtiveness and clandestinity – makes inevitable . . .'

The only answer to excesses and exploitation, homosexual as well as heterosexual, they concluded, is a more responsible and less selfish expression of sexuality. To do it is all right, but not promiscuously and not exploitatively, which means no sadomasochism, paedophilia or cruising.

Should the gay Christian aim for fidelity in a relationship? If new rules are to be drawn, should some of the old be abandoned? The American Jesuit, John McNeill, author of *Homosexuality and the Church*, conjectures that fidelity in heterosexual marriage is based on fear. 'I don't know a single gay person who would want it,' he says. Father McNeill is a psychotherapist and counsellor in New York. He was silenced by the Church after the publication of his book, not for its contents, which had been approved by the Jesuit office in Rome and bore the imprimatur, but for its success, which brought him a publicity tour and appearance on television chat shows. The Church felt that McNeill was creating the false illusion that it was about to change its teaching on homosexuality.

He does not leave the Church, because 'I love the Church. It is me and I am it.' The terms of his silencing mean that he can speak on any subject that does not involve sexual ethics. He will observe privately, however, that priests still urge young men troubled by their leanings to get married; that the Church, with its impossible sexual codes, has weakened the dependence on authority and has caused Catholics to rely on personal conscience; and that what heterosexuals can learn from homosexuals is that there are some duties that come from equality, not from procreation.

When fidelity becomes a formal issue is in the wording of the services of blessing that many religious gay couples wish to have performed. The services are controversial, even though organizations like the British Gay Christian Movement cannot see why: 'Presumably if clergy can bless battleships and budgerigars, we can bless two men or two women who are in love and wish to make solemn vows to each other.' Needless to say, there are no Catholic ceremonies of blessing. The Pope was shocked during his American visit in 1979 even to hear some Catholic priests suggesting that they might be desirable. Yet clergymen of lenient denominations, like the Unitarian Universalists, as well as known sympathetic individual clergymen in other Protestant churches, are receiving more and more requests for blessings for same-sex unions.

Why do not these couples just go out into the woods or hills, find some beautiful spot and make their vows to each other there? The Rev. Robert Wheatly, a gay Unitarian minister, who has performed many such ceremonies, asks them. 'No. We want a ceremony,' they reply. He has his own answer. 'Because people need each other.' Most of the requests come from lesbian couples. 'It isn't surprising,' Mr Wheatly says, 'this further proof of the difference between men and women. Women want to make commitments in general. Men don't.'

Couples from all kinds of religious backgrounds – Catholic, Protestant, Greek Orthodox – come to the Unitarian doors for this ritual their own churches will not give them.

What then, should an institution, even one as flexible as the Unitarian Church, require in the way of conditions to be met before a service is merited? A minimum time together? A lifetime promise? Mr Wheatly looks for some sense of the couple wanting to make a public statement and for some sign that they are serious in their intention. He does not expect them to promise fidelity or to remain together for ever. Unitarianism is more open that that. 'I try to help them to express outwardly what they feel inwardly about their commitment, about their goals, about their love for each other. A commitment for love, as long as love shall last.' The emotion and pride that are poured into these ceremonies of blessing astonish him, even though he has performed many. One of the most moving was two Irish-Catholic boys from South Boston, only nineteen and twenty, with names that might well have been Pat and Mike. They presented themselves to him asking for a service. They planned all the details very carefully and counted the days. They had an empty apartment where they were going to live and they decided the ceremony should take place there.

'I went down there with my eyes popping out – that this should be taking place, in that Irish-Catholic stronghold! And there was nothing secret about it. They had their friends and relatives there to watch. Their landlord – he's straight, but they wanted him to share in the ceremony – suddenly had to go to the hospital. So we decided to have the blessing of the rings in his hospital room. There he lay in bed, drinking beer, with visitors around and we all gathered and blessed the rings. Then back at the apartment we had the ceremony itself.

'One of their cousins, a woman, said to me, "This isn't for real, is it? It's just make-believe."

'"It is real," I said. "It just isn't legal."'

There are homosexual couples who decide to remain chaste until the ceremony. In an account of one such agreement published by the Gay Christian Movement, Sue Jex said to Sara Coggin, after they had become engaged: 'Do you mind if we wait until we can have some kind of blessing service?' Then they had to choose the form of words to use:

'Sexual fidelity was not an issue for us as we both assumed it, but I had to ask whether either of us was really in a position to promise to love each other until death. Unlike Sue, I had been in a relationship before, and then it had been me who had insisted on a promise of permanence. I had no desire to face the sorrow of a broken relationship again, yet the previous two years had forced me to accept that loving sometimes involves letting the other go to journey in another direction . . . Eventually we agreed on

177

the formula, "as long as God wills", and the natural insecurity which Sue felt has been removed by the deepening love of our life together.'

After the service, 'we emerged into the dappled September sunshine, deeply happy. Back at home, my two-year-old niece presented her two "aunties" with a gift and my brother-in-law photographed us cutting the cake.'

The Gay Christian Movement offers several alternative designs of service, for what it considers solemn vows, not taken or renounced lightly. If the pair wishes to promise fidelity, the following dialogue is suggested:

> PRIEST: 'Will you swear to remain faithful to each other, never allowing any other relationship to come before the one you are now to affirm?'
> COUPLE: 'We will . . .'
> Each partner then makes her/his Vow to the other, taking his/her right hand and saying:
> 'I, N, vow you, M, in the sight of God and before these our chosen witnesses, that I shall love, honour and cherish you all the days of my life until death divides us.'

The priest then blesses the rings which are exchanged; they pray, the priest blesses them and asks the congregation to make a vow to support them. There are more prayers and blessings and hymns; the congregation signs a commemorative card which is given to the couple, the priest leads the prayers for the couple, and, if wanted, there is communion.

If the promise is not wanted or if the couple have not known each other very long, a simple 'Prayer for a Couple' is suggested, to be said by the minister and the two people concerned, in the privacy of the study, home or chapel. The literal promise of sexual fidelity can be sidestepped with:

> MINISTER: 'Do you promise to be loyal to each other, never allowing any other relationship to come before the one you are now to affirm?'

or,

> 'Your relationship has not yet been tested by time or trouble. Will you try to make it a strong and permanent one?'
> COUPLE: 'We will.'

Gay Christians will not rest until the church of their choice recognizes that it is entirely compatible with the Christian faith not only to love another person of the same sex but also to express that love sexually.

The board for social responsibility of the Church of England went that far in its report, approving stable homosexual relationships, and in some circumstances ordination to the priesthood. Nonetheless, it plunged the Anglican church into one of those furores about sex and morals that its tolerant liberalism almost seems to court. The Archbishop of Canterbury, leader of the worldwide Episcopalian and Anglican community, was moved to say that he does not believe that homosexual practices are acceptable within the Christian moral tradition.

The way out of the dilemma for the churches is to stop looking at sex in legalistic terms of specific acts and rather to place greater emphasis on the dignity and quality of the personal relationship surrounding sex. In that sense Pope John Paul's statement that a man can be guilty of adultery with his own wife was actually helpful. Yet the higher status awarded married love will be hard to shift, even after homosexuality itself is more understood and accepted. The phrase used by the American Episcopal House of Bishops in rejecting homosexuality was that it constituted a 'witness to incompleteness'.

The Christian concept of marriage is that it symbolizes the mystical union between Christ and his Church, or, put in more anthropological terms, between divinity and humanity. In other words, marriage is a metaphor for the union of opposites – of self and other, of male and female, not of like and like.

For homosexuals unconcerned with religion, this concept of the meaning of marriage merely justifies their own belief that homosexual sex belongs outside the conventional moral code. It is something on its own, they argue: sex that is sterile but also harmless, practised for release and recreation, incapable of causing unwanted pregnancies, death by childbirth, the passage of property to other than the legitimate heir or any other of the social ills that the

Judaeo-Christian sexual ethic was designed (inefficiently) to restrain. The same rules simply do not need to apply.

Those who want their gayness and God too are going to have a long struggle. They are asking that the churches, which are by nature conservative, give up their interest in the personal life of their clergymen and change their philosophy of the purpose of marriage. For full equality under the sacraments, gay Christians may have to wait until easier questions are settled first, like the ordination of women and the gender of God.

13

Acts of Union

What attitude should society take towards male homosexual promiscuity? That is the only moral question left in homosexuality for anyone who accepts that a substantial fraction of the population is drawn to its own sex with the same intensity as the majority is to the opposite sex, and who can see that homosexuals have no prerogative in seducing the young. Yet the relentless cruising, the penchant for anonymous partners, the take-over of public places for selfish use cannot be anything but offensive to ordinary standards of dignity of the individual and of sex as communication.

The extent of male homosexual promiscuity has not been exaggerated. The Kinsey Institute stated this fact baldly. What it found in San Francisco confirmed earlier studies and provided new figures based on a very large sample. The average male subject, according to the Institute, had had more than 500 sexual partners in his lifetime. Of the white males in the study, 28 per cent reported more than a thousand. Such frenetic impersonal encounters are the very opposite of gay and are just what legal and social acceptance of homosexuality was supposed to reduce.

Given this evidence, gay spokesmen will often reply that society needs no 'attitude' – least of all condescending tolerance. They want it to accord gay behaviour the same moral neutrality as any other sexual activity between consenting adults. Yet at the same time they can offer an explanation for the phenomenon. It is that homosexual promiscuity is no more than quintessential maleness – the way that all men would behave if women would only let them. Who knows how promiscuous heterosexual men are, they ask, and who could answer? Scores are not easy to come by – many have long lost count – but men do boast of conquests into the hundreds, a boast not confined to the present day. In the opera *Don Giovanni*, Mozart has Leporello singing out his insatiable master's lifetime count of ladies loved – two thousand and sixty-five.

This 'men are like that' argument was set forward in the journal, *Family Coordinator*, by Bruce Voeller. Asked to explain why homosexual men were much less monogamous than homosexual women, he replied:

> There is a clear double standard. Men, whether homosexual or heterosexual, are socialized in our society to be sexual. Women, on the other hand, are socialized to deny their sexual feelings, or to be ashamed of them. The consequences of putting two [gay] men together in our society – each socialized as a male to seek sexual relationships aggressively – is a high coupling probability. However, when you put a man and a woman together, the woman is much more likely to deny or reject those sexual feelings, with a resulting lower probability of consummating a sexual encounter than for two men.
>
> In the case of two women in a lesbian relationship, both women have been socialized as women to reject their sexual feelings for each other, and the probability of their having a sexual encounter is less than in either case where males are involved. Thus, when you have a hard-gained relationship between two women, it's more likely that it will be carefully nurtured.

Voeller concluded:

> homosexual men are probably not more promiscuous but merely more successful in their sexual efforts than heterosexual men, given the like-mindedness of their quarry.

Whatever the explanation, sexual scores well up to the Kinsey San Francisco level were acknowledged (along with the predictable consequences) by many of the homosexual men who volunteered for this book. To take a typical comment:

'How many partners have I had? It's got to be hundreds. I'm forty-seven years of age. Two or three times I've had binges . . . I don't know what the total numbers would be. Any VD? Oh, yes. I have a wonderful doctor. Most gays in New York do. I have to constantly watch, as most gays do, for amoebic dysentery especially. It comes up from the islands. You are aware of the signals. I just call my doctor. He's gay. As you walk into his office, he's literally got the syringe ready to take blood. He says if you have sex only with one person and know they're not having sex with anyone else, you've nothing to worry about. Otherwise, you should have periodic checkups.'

The easiest social response to this kind of behaviour is utter revulsion. That was the judgement delivered by Midge Decter in her *Commentary* blast against gay liberation. To have had more than 500 lovers, she said, quoting the Kinsey statistic, 'bespeaks the obliteration of all experience, if not, indeed, of oneself'. She went on:

> To become homosexual is a weighty act. Taking oneself out of the tides of ordinary mortal existence is not something one does from any longings to think oneself ordinary . . . Gay Lib has been an effort to set the weight of that act at naught, to define homosexuality as nothing more than a casual option among options . . . [Faced with] the accelerating round of drugs, S-M and suicide, can either the [Gay Lib] movement or its heterosexual sympathizers imagine that they have done anyone a kindness?

Midge Decter did not suggest what form kindness to homosexuals might take. Helping them to keep out of sight? Fighting the repeal of sodomy laws? Encouraging police to resume their old practice of peeping through holes in the walls of public lavatories? Clearly, some more reflective response is required than lumping all homosexuals together as try-anything beachboys, considering the main finding of the Kinsey Institute's formidable San Francisco work – that there is as great a variety of ways of living as a homosexual as of a heterosexual.

Any genuine attempt to suggest new and constructive social policies towards homosexuality has to take into account the kind of stable homosexual pair labelled by the Kinsey Institute as 'close-coupled'. Their anxieties have nothing to do with mascara or whips and leather, more to do with the lack of social recognition for love.

Robert and Russell are a couple who intend to spend the rest of their lives with each other. In their early thirties, they have been together for four years. They are buying a house. While they do not see themselves in man-and-wife roles, Russell does have an engineering degree and a good salary, so they put his career first. Robert tries to find a job wherever Russell's is. They share the cooking, Robert chooses the furnishings, Russell looks after both cars. As time goes on, they think the bonds between them are stronger than ever. The only really rough time they had was when Russell was working in Wales and Robert stayed in their old flat in Berkshire, with Russell coming home weekends. The first night would be wonderful. The next day they'd be on edge. The third they'd argue, then Russell would have to go back. That separation did them no good.

In their circle are quite a few stable homosexual couples. While some have been together for thirty years, they know they are in the minority. All of them tell Robert and Russell, 'You must stay together. There is so much envy of stable relationships in the gay world that people will try to break you up just out of jealousy.' The two men have more or less given up going to gay bars. Some people make a profession of being gay. That's something they don't agree with.

Are they faithful? Yes, oh yes. Entirely, touch wood. It's a small price to pay for a very happy relationship. They know they have something rare, something to be proud of.

Legally they have gone as far as they can to make a permanent bond. They are buying their house in their joint names. They have made their wills so as to leave everything to each other. Eventually they are going to look into fostering to try and have some children around; they might invite a woman friend whose husband has virtually deserted her to move in, with her two children. Being homosexual should not make you radical, say Robert and Russell.

Yet public taboos do serve to undermine the stability of such homosexual relationships. A lesbian schoolteacher speaks of the constant pressure: 'You have to be so circumspect. If there's a misunderstanding, a slight argument in public, if it was a fellow, you could touch, or hold hands, to help make it up. We have to wait until we get home.'

For homosexual lovers of long standing who are not publicly recognized, agony can be piled upon grief when one of them dies. They are not next of kin. The survivor often cannot ask for time off to go to the funeral. He or she may be evicted from the home they shared or may not be allowed near the deathbed by relatives who may have suspected that there was something fishy about 'those two'. One woman – call her Mrs Mason – is a lesbian who still lives with her husband, as non-speaking strangers, on a council estate they cannot afford to leave. Her life had been centred on a woman friend, Lorraine, whom she loved for twenty years and with whom she had spent all her holidays. Lorraine's parents never acknowledged that their daughter was lesbian, and indeed had not needed to: for them she was a spinster living at home. One day Mrs Mason telephoned and asked to speak to her friend. 'She's dead,' Lorraine's mother said and hung up.

Mrs Mason did not know when or how or why. In shock, she called back, yet the family would give no information. 'One thing Lorraine had that I desperately wanted was a scrapbook she had made out of all the photographs we had taken on our trips together. I didn't have a single photograph of her myself. She had put them all in our book. Finally, after about three weeks, I got up the courage to call her family again and ask if I might have the book to keep as a souvenir of our friendship . . . or at least a few of the pictures. They said they didn't know where the book was. I never heard from them again.'

There was not a single person in the world to whom Mrs Mason could confide her grief, except her doctor. He had always been sympathetic; his son is gay, she thinks, that would explain it. He offered her some tranquillizers. She was reluctant. 'Take them,' he said. 'You need them, after what you've been through.'

Making a home together is the commonest and most satisfying way that homosexual couples can express their wish for permanence. A business executive is earnest, girlish in the best sense, about the hopes he has for the house he and his lover are renovating: 'This is my first house. My friend is six or seven years younger than me and earns less than I do. Perhaps I'll pay for the wood to make the bookshelves and my friend will invest the labour of shaping the wood into shelves. But I'm into communities now as well as relationships. I want to get along with the neighbours. I might want to leave the key with them some time, for example. I don't want anonymity. I want us to be recognized as a couple.'

There is one contribution society could make to homosexual stability: to allow people of the same sex to marry. Surely if homosexual equality means anything, it means equality under the laws. If millions of heterosexuals find order and happiness in the legal status called marriage, why should the same legal advantages be denied to millions of other people because of their sexual preference?

Let one thing be clear. To say that the proposal for same-sex marriage does not interest many in the gay rights movement is to put it mildly. They pour out scorn at the very mention of the word, usually by using the verb 'to ape'.

'It is a nasty idea. Simply aping heterosexual marriage.'

'You can be exclusively faithful without a piece of paper.'

'That's one of the advantages of being gay – you are more attuned to the idea of sharing.'

To homosexual theoreticians, gay liberation is a radical movement, breaking with bourgeois institutions of all kinds. Marriage is one of those from which they are privileged to be free. They dislike the property element in marriage; listen, they say, to the words of the ceremony, which are as much about 'worldly goods' as about 'keeping only unto each other'. Fidelity and monogamy in themselves amount to ownership of bodies – another concept they reject.

The reasoned case against marriage is well put by a thoughtful lesbian, who is in her late thirties and who has no intention of leaving her lover: 'Marriage is probably useful for some couples. It would not be for me, in personal terms or in any legalized societal terms. I don't feel a lack of emotional commitment or willingness to make it. While I am very much opposed to musical beds, overconfidence in a relationship can be a trap. I see a lot of people, women, settling in and taking their relationship for granted and I can see that they have set the lid on the coffin of that relationship.

'My partner and I aren't even interested in living together. I've been involved with other people where you did everything together but your laundry. Private time is important to me, and to Christine. I'm not in touch with my own feelings and thoughts if I've no time to myself. She has her apartment and I have mine. We see each other a couple of times a week but we can spend periods of time away from each other. Frankly, it's the best relationship I've ever been involved in. I help her and she turns around and helps me.

'We own just one thing together, a winter jacket – blue, with inner lining. It was a wonderful buy in Harrods sale. Fifteen pounds. She had seven and I had eight. We toss for wearing it.'

For those who want it and can sustain it, such independence is fine. Yet many homosexuals, for reasons that have nothing to do with religion, yearn for some version of legal marriage. Some are almost crying for it. A girl at the switchboard of a homophile organization, simply upon hearing the possibility mentioned, broke in, 'Oh, do they allow it now? I would just love to be able to get married to my partner!' Some divorced homosexuals who found the institution of marriage important when they were in it would like something comparable when they go gay. One such man living with his lover declared passionately: 'If there were some form of marriage ceremony available, we would go through it like a shot. There's something tangible about being paired – a firm and binding declaration which two people very much need.'

Pathetic? Comic? Read on. Here are extracts from the ceremony of commitment that two young professionals from

Manhattan wrote for themselves to speak before friends in lieu of a wedding. Each composed his own terms, according to his own feelings:

ALLEN: 'At a certain point in a relationship between a man and woman, society's protection is invoked on that relationship by the act of marriage. That act is not now available to two men who wish to make a commitment to each other. Gay people are not bound by the forms of straight society, but we also lack certain of the supports offered by that society.

'The purpose of this Statement of Commitment is to invoke the protection of our community on our Act of Commitment. So, in the presence of fellow gay people, I, Allen, make the following Statement of Commitment to you, Brian.

1. I commit myself to be your sexual partner.
2. I commit myself to be your companion.
3. I commit myself to be your friend.

'It would be neat to stop with three items. But life is often less than neat. Even though I violate my own symmetry, let me make some additional promises:

A. I promise to respect you, your space and your things.
B. I promise to restrain my own selfishness.
C. We have previously discussed certain ground rules of our living together; without outlining them here, I promise to follow those rules.
D. I promise to be supportive of you both when requested and when not requested.
E. I promise to wear and cherish such ring or other evidence of our love as we may agree upon.

'I make these promises out of deep love and respect for you. Aristotle defined friendship as "One soul abiding in two bodies". I pledge in my commitment to you to let the spirit of that definition be my guide.'

BRIAN: 'It is rare. It is unbelievable. It is uncommon. And yet somehow I feel it is not unlikely that the two of us would, could and will continue to discover each other. I trust you. I believe in you. Gay couples often find they must depend on each other more than heterosexual couples feel compelled to do. We must find new internal strengths that delve beyond what most people call patience and concern and we must build together . . .

'I am committed to building a family with you and your kids. I am committed to supporting your ambitions and

188

goals and your right to be the kind of person you want to be and to work towards goals you want for yourself. I am committed to believing that you and I as gay people have the right to express the depth and strength of our relationship just as straight people do and will work towards that goal in our lifetime.'

If it were ever to be permitted, same-sex marriage would require a revolutionary change in the legal meaning of marriage. Through the ages, the contract of marriage has had one fundamental requirement – that the couple consist of one male and one female: a reproductive pair at least in theory. No matter if the couple are in their eighties. Nor if they have sexual organs that are damaged or non-existent. They do not have to know each other or to be present at their own wedding (Ingrid Bergman and Roberto Rossellini were in Rome when they were married by proxy in Mexico City in 1950). They may be on their deathbeds. But as long as they are not related by any of the degrees of kindred in the categories forbidden by the law in the place where they marry, and as long as they are not married to anyone else and are above the legal age limit, they may marry each other. Nothing in the words of their contract obliges them to make any commitment to children. Their commitment is to each other.

In fact, a beginning in the erosion of the traditional rules has already been made by the rise in sex-change surgery. Transsexuals, who have altered sex, frequently seek to marry. One of the first was the English model, April Ashley. When she tried to take out a marriage licence, she was refused permission. A court ruled that for purposes of marrying, it is not the doctor's certificate but the birth certificate that counts. Born males may only marry born females – in Britain. Elsewhere the rules vary wildly but tend towards prohibition. Transsexuals may marry in New Jersey, Norway, South Africa and the province of Alberta. In Denmark, the decision is based on the merits of individual cases.

However, the outright marriage between people of the same sex does not seem to be recognized anywhere, not even in Denmark or Holland which are noted for their liberal treatment of homosexuals. According to John Boswell, ancient Rome permitted the practice, but his examples are few. It is true that for a brief period in 1975 county clerks in the state of Colorado did issue marriage licences to homosexual couples and much of the present vague belief that 'homosexual marriage' is possible somewhere is based on that event. However, these 'marriages' were declared invalid, first in a ruling by the Colorado Attorney General; then, in a test case in California, brought by a male couple seeking to use the Colorado precedent to validate their own attempt at marriage.

This California case (Adams v. Howerton) clearly illustrates the legal advantage of the married state. It was brought by two men, one American, one Australian, who had gone through a marriage ceremony in order to save the Australian from deportation. Together, the couple claimed that their constitutional rights to equal treatment under the law was violated because, by being threatened with expulsion from the US, the Australian was not being treated as the American's spouse or immediate relative by virtue of marriage. Thus stated, the case gave the US District Court for Central California an opportunity to take a look at the federal law's concept of the purpose of marriage. The opinion issued by the federal judge provides a clear summary of the law's justification for excluding same-sex couples but not infertile couples from the right to marry.

Even if the Colorado Attorney General had ruled that same-sex marriages were legal in that state, said the judge, his words would not have mattered, for if a state law should offend federal public policy, it is federal policy that prevails. That policy, he said, was spelled out most clearly in the case of Singer v. Hara: 'Marriage exists as a protected legal institution primarily because of societal values associated with the propagation of the human race.' The judge went on to observe that English civil law, based on both Judaic and Christian laws, has held for centuries that marriage is impossible and unthinkable between persons of the same sex. In the light of this tradition, the judge ruled, 'It seems

190

clear to me that Congress, as a matter of federal law, did not intend that a person of one sex could be a "spouse" to a person of the same sex for immigration purposes . . .' He dismissed the couple's claim to be married and also to have been denied their constitutional rights. Then he tackled the underlying philosophical question.

Why, he proposed, if some persons are allowed to marry even though the legally stated justification for marriage – procreation – is not possible, should not all couples for whom procreation is impossible be allowed the same right? Then he framed his answer as follows:

> In my opinion, if the classification of the group who may validly marry is overinclusive, it does not affect the validity of the classification. In traditional equal-protection terminology, it seems beyond dispute that the state has a compelling interest in encouraging and fostering procreation of the race and providing status and stability to the environment in which children are raised. There is no real alternative to overbreadth in achieving this goal . . . The alternative would be to inquire of each couple, before issuing a marriage licence, as to their plans for children and to give sterility tests to all applicants, refusing licences to those found sterile or unwilling to raise a family. Such tests and inquiries would themselves raise serious constitutional questions . . . Thus, it seems to me that the state has chosen the least intrusive alternative available to protect the procreative relationship.

How long this legal position – overbreadth in the interests of procreation – can be held will be worth watching. The American Civil Liberties Union has undertaken to examine whether the refusal to permit homosexuals to marry constitutes deprivation of equality under the law. Sooner or later, however, realism will demand that marriage be redefined to reduce or eliminate its emphasis on reproduction and to emphasize society's sustained interest in legal public commitment. What marriage ought to become is a contract, publicly announced, for two people to stay together and to be considered a unit for as long as they both desire it.

This change should be made, rather than the abolition of

marriage altogether, because the most ignored fact of the sexual revolution is the continuing popularity of marriage. Reports of the death of marriage and the family have been premature. All that has died is the shotgun wedding; it is a rare girl who 'has to get married' any more. When novel changes in living patterns are publicized, like the increase in living together or living alone, they serve to obscure the massive conservatism of the habits of the majority. The world is still dominated by married people. For each of the liberated individuals who declares that the legal and economic underpinnings of marriage are irrelevant to the world that is emerging, there are others deciding to get that 'piece of paper', and they routinely include many couples who have lived together unmarried for years. Census statistics show that three-quarters of American households still are headed by a married couple. Two-thirds of these have been married only once, to each other. Although that proportion will drop, the main demographic pattern will not alter very much by 1990. Even by then, moreover, the census predicts that 56 per cent of all children will still be living in families headed by married couples. Married life for many, therefore will remain the ideal and it would be surprising if some of those who do not enter it or who grow up in one-parent families do not continue to have wistful dreams about what they may be missing.

In reality, as divorce and unmarried cohabitation increase, marriage itself will take on greater significance as a way of establishing family ties for a child, out and beyond its pair of parents. For a child whose parents have remarried, for example, grandparents take on a double function – as surrogate parents and as landmarks of biological origin. If homosexual couples could be permitted to marry, they would be able to become affinal relatives – aunts, uncles and stepparents – to children in their spouse's family.

Any campaign to legalize same-sex marriage would be bound to arouse controversy at least as great as that over legalizing abortion. The Mary Whitehouse corner of public opinion prefers homosexuals to remain, in Midge Decter's words, 'out of the tides of ordinary mortal existence'. Yet as a step in the extension of civil liberties to minorities, same-sex marriage is just as logical and fair as any other of the reforms that have been granted in the past decade or two. One possible way to achieve it might be through the introduction of two forms, or tiers, of marriage. Dr Mia Kellmer Pringle, former director of the British National Children's Bureau, has suggested two-tier marriage as a way of reconciling society's wish for quick and easy divorce with its need to provide a stable home for children. A simple form of marriage licence would be available for couples without children. For those who wanted children, however, a more binding contract, lasting ten to fifteen years, would be required. The first form could easily suit homosexual couples, and the second might as well, for those wanting to adopt.

In lieu of marriage, homosexuals are increasingly turning to the non-marital agreement, the private contract, in the wake of the initial decision in the Lee Marvin case: the Californian Supreme Court ruled in 1979 that Marvin and his former mistress had developed an implied contract in seven years of living together, with contractual property rights similar to those of married couples. Since then, dozens of law suits have been filed by people seeking a share of the assets of someone with whom they have ceased to live. The most celebrated of these cases was brought by a woman who was formerly secretary to Billie Jean King. Now, even though the Marvin decision was blurred on appeal, it has become clear to many couples that a deliberate contract is better than an implicit one. To forestall law suits if they were to split up, they began taking the trouble to spell out their agreed rights and obligations to each other. Unlike marriage, such a contract can be drawn up for a limited period and then renegotiated. However, as a review in the *Washington Blade*, a gay newspaper, pointed out, homosexual couples are deceiving themselves if they think that such written agreements are sure to be upheld everywhere. As California law goes, so do courts in many more conservative states try to go in the opposite direction.

For homosexual couples who want legal backing for their

relationship, the Lambda Legal Defense and Education Fund has suggested some steps they should consider taking: joint ownership of stocks, bonds and bank accounts (but keeping an eye out for the possibility of having to pay gift tax); giving each other power of attorney; telling their doctors that each other is to be treated as next of kin; putting both names on the lease of a shared flat or house; making wills, and leaving instructions to each other for funeral and burial.

Yet none of the arrangements carries the public recognition of the couple as a couple that, to many heterosexuals, is the most satisfying benefit of being married. Perhaps only when homosexuals have a comparable right to set up community-recognized households will many of them abandon the promiscuity that causes the heterosexual world to reject them. It took centuries for society to drop the absurd legal shackles of 'fornication' and 'lewd and lascivious cohabitation' and to allow men and women who wanted to live together the freedom not to marry. What needs fighting for now is an expansion of the freedom to marry.

If that right is to be gained for homosexual couples, however, the need for a new demographic study of the sweeping scope of the original Kinsey reports is urgent. Certainly not until homosexuals are recognized in something like their true numbers in Britain will they get equal treatment under the law. The same argument that the census uses to persuade other minorities not to evade answering – that there are financial and social advantages to their whole group in being counted accurately – applies to them. It is unlikely that 'sexual preference or orientation' will ever need to appear on a census form. But if Kinsey could find a valid way of estimating the proportion of homosexuals in the population in the 1940s, when homosexuality still could not speak its name, something more precise must be possible today. Too many people believe that they have never seen a homosexual except on television.

As the stereotypes of homosexuality continue to recede and as homosexuals realize that there are alternatives to a

194

life of desperate loneliness, fewer should fall into aimless promiscuity or unworkable marriages. If the gay movement wants that change to occur, however, it must somehow take into its demands the right to be a parent. At present, it gives insufficient recognition to the wish for paternity. It must also be more sympathetic to married homosexuals, who are now the outcasts of both gay and straight societies.

Some gay-straight marriages are not shameful compromises between the two worlds, but good marriages by any standards. A young lesbian from San Francisco insists, 'I think gay people should get married. Marriage is how the sexes should live together.' An old trade unionist from Manchester, a closeted gay, now widowed, says, 'I had my arms around her when she died. She never knew. But it wasn't a strain keeping it from her. I've loved and not lost. I couldn't run off. We were married forty-two years. She was a wonderful wife to me.' Nigel Nicolson, writing of his parents, Harold Nicolson and Vita Sackville-West, called their story a 'panegyric of marriage' because 'each found permanent and undiluted happiness only in the company of the other. If their marriage is seen as a harbour, their love affairs were mere ports of call; it was there that both were based.'

Same-sex marriage, were it to become legal, would be unlikely to bring an end to homosexuals marrying heterosexuals for there will always remain more people in the middle of the Kinsey scale than at the exclusively homosexual extreme and many of these will resolve their ambivalence by choosing the course that looks able to fulfil the vision of family life that dances in all our heads, cosy, warm and burnished as a Dutch interior. It may be that gayness, as the homosexual movement says, is incompatible with traditional marriage. Yet there may also be a complementarity between the sexes that transcends sex and draws them to each other. As Ford Madox Ford wrote in *The Good Soldier*, the story of two passionless marriages:

> For, whatever may be said of the relation of the sexes, there is no man who loves a woman that does not desire to come to her for the renewal of his courage, for the cutting asunder of his

difficulties . . . We are all so afraid, we are all so alone, we all so need from the outside the assurance of our own worthiness to exist.

Gay liberation is too recent for anyone to know whether or not homosexuals will lose their interest in marrying hetero-sexuals. At present, it is evident that many homosexuals, in or out of the closet, male or female, feel that two sexes are needed to make a home and that marriage is their goal, if only they can find the right person.

Bibliography

Altman, Dennis, *Homosexual Oppression and Liberation*. London: Allen Lane, 1971.

Arce, Hector, *The Secret Life of Tyrone Power*. New York: William Morrow & Co., 1979.

Baker, Robb, *Bette Midler*. London: Angus & Robertson, 1980.

Bancroft, John *et al.*, 'The Control of Deviant Sexual Behaviour by Drugs', *British Journal of Psychiatry* 125 (1974): 310–15.

Barnett, Leonard, *Homosexuality: Time to Tell the Truth*. London: Gollancz, 1975.

Barringe, Felicity and Boodman, Sandra G., 'Congressman's Revelation', *Washington Post*, 9 August 1980.

Beauvoir, Simone de, *The Second Sex*. London: Cape, 1953.

Bell, Alan P., and Weinberg, Martin S., *Homosexualities: A Study of Diversity Among Men and Women*. New York: Simon & Schuster, 1978.

Bell, Quentin, *Virginia Woolf*, vol. 1. London: Hogarth Press, 1972.

Beye, Charles R., *Ancient Greek Literature and Society*. New York: Anchor Press, 1975.

Bieber, Irving, *Homosexuality: A Psychoanalytic Study of Male Homosexuals*. New York: Basic Books, 1962.

Bieber, Toby B., 'Acting Out in Homosexuality', in *Acting Out*, edited by L. E. Abt and S. L. Weissman. New York: Jason Aronson, 1976.

Birk, Lee, 'Group Psychotherapy for Men who are Homosexual', *Journal of Sex and Marital Therapy* 1 (1974).

Birk, Lee, 'The Myth of Classical Homosexuality: View of a Behavioural Psychotherapist', in *Homosexual Behaviour*, edited by Judd Marmor. New York: Basic Books, 1980.

Birk, Lee and Brinkley-Birk, Ann, 'Case Report of Learning Therapies', *Psychiatric Opinion* 12, March 1975.

Birk, Lee, Miller, Elizabeth and Cohler, Bertram, 'Group Psychotherapy for Homosexual Men', *Acta Psychiatrica Scandinavica*, Suppl. 218 (1970).

Boswell, John, *Christianity, Social Tolerance and Homosexuality*. Chicago: The University of Chicago Press, 1980.

Brody, Jane E. 'Kinsey Study Finds Homosexuals Show Deep Predisposition', *New York Times*, 23 August 1981.

Catholic Social Welfare Commission, *An Introduction to the Pastoral Care of Homosexual People*. Abbots Langley, Hertfordshire: Catholic Information Services, 1979.

Chambers, Whittaker, FBI interview, 18 February 1949, FBI Document 2152.

Chambers, Whittaker, *Witness*. New York: Random House, 1952.

Chippindale, Peter and Leigh, David, *The Thorpe Committal*. London: Arrow Books, 1979.

Colette, *Earthly Paradise: An Autobiography*. London: Secker & Warburg, 1966.

Cooper, Emmanuel, 'Duncan Grant', *Gay News*, 6 March 1980.

Davison, Gerald C., 'Not Can But Ought: The Treatment of Homosexuality', *Journal of Consulting and Clinical Psychology*, Vol. 46, No. 1, 170–72.

Decter, Midge, 'The Boys on the Beach', *Commentary*, September 1980.

'Don't Blame Me, I Was Drunk', *Newsweek*, 20 October 1980.

Driberg, Tom, *Ruling Passions*. London: Jonathan Cape, 1977.

Duberman, Martin B., Review of *Homosexuality in Perspective*, by William H. Masters and Virginia E. Johnson *The New Republic*, 16 June 1979.

Edel, Leon, *Bloomsbury: A House of Lions*. London: Hogarth Press, 1979.

Engels, Frederick, *The Origin of the Family, Private Property and the State*. London: Lawrence & Wishart, 1972.

Ettorre, E. M., *Lesbians, Women and Society*. London: Routledge & Kegan Paul, 1980.

Faber, Doris, *The Life of Lorena Hickok*. New York: William Morrow & Co., 1980.

Family Law Report, Admas v. Howerton: USDG C Calif, 25/2/80, G FLR 2338–40, 3 March 1980.

Firestone, Shulamith, *The Dialectic of Sex*. London: Cape, 1971.

Ford, Ford Madox, *The Good Soldier*. London: Penguin Books, 1946.

Frank, Jerome D., 'Treatment of Homosexuals', in *Final Report of the Task Force on Homosexuality*. Rockville, Md: National Institute of Mental Health, 1972.

Freud, Sigmund, 'Letter to an American Mother', *Letters of Sigmund Freud, 1873–1939*. London: Hogarth Press, 1970.

Furbank, P. N., *E. M. Forster: A Life*. London: Secker & Warburg, 1977 and 1978.

Gebhard, Paul H., 'Incidence of Overt Homosexuality in the United States and Western Europe', in *Final Report of the Task Force on Homosexuality*. Rockville, Md.: National Institute of Mental Health, 1972.

Gilson, Étienne, *The Spirit of Medieval Philosophy*. New York: Scribner's, 1940.

Glick, Paul, 'Children of Divorced Parents in Demographic Perspective', *Journal of Social Issues* 34, (1979).

Glick, Paul C., 'Married and Unmarried Cohabitation in the United States', *Journal of Marriage and the Family*, February 1980.

Glick, Paul C., 'Remarriage: Some Recent Changes and Variations', *Journal of Family Issues* 1, December 1980.

Glick, Paul C., and Norton, Arthur J., 'Marrying, Divorcing and Living Together in the US Today', *Population Bulletin* 32, February 1979.

Green, Dr Richard, 'Sexual Identity of 37 Children Raised by Homosexual or Transsexual Parents', *American Journal of Psychiatry*, 135, 6 June 1978.

Groth, Nicholas A. and Birnbaum, Jean, H., 'Adult Sexual Orientation and Attraction to Underage Persons', *Archives of Sexual Behaviour* 7, May 1978, 175–81.

Hatterer, Lawrence J., *Changing Homosexuality in the Male*. New York: McGraw Hill Book Co., 1970.

Hatterer, Lawrence J., *The Pleasure Addicts*. New York: A. S. Barnes & Co., 1980.

Higham, Charles, *Charles Laughton*. London: W. H. Allen & Co., 1976.

Hocquehem, Guy, *Homosexual Desire*. London: Allison & Busby, 1978.

Holleran, Andrew, *Dancer from the Dance*. New York: Bantam Books, 1980.

Holroyd, Michael, 'Looking Back at Bloomsbury'. *The Times*, 1 March, 1980.

Holroyd, Michael, *Lytton Strachey: The Unknown Years, 1880–1910* and *Lytton Strachey: The Years of Achievement, 1910–1932*. London: Heinemann, 1967 and 1968.

Honoré, Tony, *Sex Law*. London: Duckworth, 1978.

Hooker, Evelyn, 'Homosexuality', in *Final Report of the Task Force on Homosexuality*. Rockville, Md.: National Institute of Mental Health, 1972.

Humphreys, Laud, *Tearoom Trade: Impersonal Sex in Public Places*. London: Duckworth, 1970.

Hunt, Morton, *Gay*. New York: Farrar, Straus & Giroux, Inc., 1977.

Hyde, H. Montgomery, *Oscar Wilde*. London: Eyre Methuen, 1976.

Hyde, H. Montgomery, *The Other Love*. London: Heinemann, 1970.

Inglis, Brian, *Roger Casement*. London: Hodder & Stoughton, 1973.

Isherwood, Christopher, *A Meeting by the River*. London: Methuen, 1967.

Jay, Karla and Young, Allen, *The Gay Report*. New York: Summit Books, 1979.

Kallman, F. J. 'Comparative Twin Study on the Genetic Aspects of Male Homosexuality', *Journal of Nervous and Mental Disease*, 115: 283–298, 1952.

Katz, Robin, 'If You Loved a Homosexual', *Honey*, September 1978.

Kearns, Doris, *Lyndon Johnson and the American Dream*. London: André Deutsch, 1976.

Keats, John, *You Might As Well Live: the Life and Times of Dorothy Parker*. London: Secker & Warburg, 1971.

Khan, M. Masud, *Alienation in Perversions*. London: Hogarth Press, 1979.

Kinsey, Alfred, C., Pomeroy, Wardell B. and Martin, Clyde

E., *Sexual Behaviour in the Humun Male*. London: W. B. Saunders, 1948.

Kinsey, Alfred C., Pomeroy, Wardell B., Martin, Clyde E. and Gebhard, Paul H., *Sexual Behaviour in the Human Female*. London: W. B. Saunders, 1953.

Kirkpatrick, Martha, Smith, Katharine and Roy, Ron, 'Adjustment and Sexual Identity of Children of Lesbian and Heterosexual Single Mothers'. *American Journal of Orthopsychiatry* vol. 51, July 1981.

Klein, Fred, MD, *The Bisexual Option*. New York: Arbor House, 1978.

Kleinberg, Seymour (ed.), *The Other Persuasion*. New York: Random House, 1977.

Lacey, W. K., *The Family in Classical Greece*. London: Thames & Hudson, 1968.

Ladurie, Emmanuel L. *Montaillou: Cathars and Catholics in a French Village 1294–1324*. London: Scolar Press, 1978.

Lahr, John, *Prick Up Your Ears: The Biography of Joe Orton*. London: Allen Lane, 1978.

Lath, J. D., and White, G. D., 'Coping with Homosexual Expression within Heterosexual Marriage', *Journal of Sex and Marital Therapy*, 4 (1978) : 198–211.

Laufer, Moses, *Adolescent Disturbance and Breakdown*. Harmondsworth Penguin Books, 1975.

'Larry and Billie Jean King Work to Renew Their Marriage – and Put Her Affair Behind Them'. *People*, 25 May, 1981.

Laurence, Ross H., 'Modes of Adjustment of Married Homosexuals', *Social Problems*, 18 (1978): 385–93.

Lawrence, D. H., *The Fox*, in *D. H. Lawrence: Short Novels*. London: Heinemann, 1956.

Levine, Edward M. and Ross, Nathaniel, 'Sexual Dysfunctions and Psychoanalysis', *American Journal of Psychiatry*, 134, 6 June 1977.

Levine, Martin, *Gay Men: The Sociology of Male Homosexuality*. New York: Harper & Row, 1979.

Levy, Paul, *Moore: G. E. Moore and the Cambridge Apostles*. London: Weidenfeld & Nicolson, 1979.

Lewin, Ellen and Lyons, Terrie, 'Lesbians and Heterosexual Mothers'. Paper for American Psychological Association, 4 September 1979.

Lewis, Debbie, 'Bisexuality: A Personal View'. *Women: A Journal of Liberation*, Winter 1974.

Linscott, Gillian, 'Lesbian Mother Wins Custody of Twins', *Guardian*, 5 November 1976.

Livingood, John M. (ed.), *Final Report of the National Institute of Mental Health Task Force on Homosexuality*. Rockville, Maryland: NIMH, 1972, DHEW Publication No. HMS 72–9/16.

Loshak, David, 'Ban on Artificial Insemination for Lesbians Rejected', *Daily Telegraph*, 27 June, 1978.

Magee, Bryan, *One in Twenty*. London: Secker & Warburg, 1966.

Marmor, Judd (ed.), *Homosexual Behaviour*. New York: Basic Books, 1980.

Marmor, Judd, 'Notes on Some Psychodynamic Aspects of Homosexuality', in *Final Report of the Task Force on Homosexuality*, Rockville, Md.: National Institute of Mental Health, 1972.

'Married Lesbians', *Sappho* 8, no. 4 (1980).

Masters, William H. and Johnson, Virginia E., *Homosexuality in Perspective*. Boston: Little, Brown & Co, 1979.

McNeill, John J., *The Church and the Homosexual*. Kansas City: Sheed, Andrews & McNeel, 1976.

Melly, George, *Owning Up*. London: Weidenfeld & Nicolson, 1975.

—, *Rum, Bum and Concertina*. London: Weidenfeld & Nicolson, 1977.

Meyers, Jeffrey, *Homosexuality and Literature*. London: Athlone Press, 1977

Miller, Brian, 'Unpromised Paternity: The Life-Styles of Gay Fathers', in *Gay Men: The Sociology of Male Homosexuality*, edited by Martin Levine. New York: Harper & Row Publishers, 1979.

Millett, Kate, *Flying*. London: Hart-Davis, MacGibbon, 1975.

Millett, Kate, *Sexual Politics*. London: Hart-Davis, MacGibbon, 1971.

'Mr Robinson and Mr Blunt', *The Times*, 22 November 1979.

Money, John, 'Sexual Dimorphism and Gender Identity', in *Final Report of the Task Force on Homosexuality*. Rockville, Md.: National Institute of Mental Health, 1972.

Morgan, Ted, *Somerset Maugham*. London: Cape, 1980.

Mosel, Tad, *Leading Lady: The World and Theatre of Katharine Cornell*. Boston: Little, Brown & Co, 1978.

Muggeridge, Malcolm, 'The Eclipse of the Gentleman', *The Times*, 3 December 1979.

National Gay Task Force, 'Gay Parent Support Pack' (New York, 1979).

Newsletter of the Bisexual Center, *The Bi-Monthly*, 3 July/August 1979.

Nicolson, Nigel, *Portrait of a Marriage*. London: Weidenfeld & Nicolson, 1973.

Office of Gay Concerns, *A Planning Guide for a Same-Sex Holy Union Ceremony*. Boston: Unitarian Universalist Association, 1978.

Pincus, Lily and Dare, Christopher, *Secrets in the Family*. London: Faber, 1978.

Pringle, Mia Kellmer, *The Needs of Children*. London: Hutchinson, 1975.

Report of the Committee on Homosexual Offences and Prostitution (Wolfenden Report). London: HMSO, Cmnd. 247, September 1957.

Rich, Adrienne, Commencement Address in *Smith Alumnae Bulletin*, Fall 1979.

Rich, Adrienne, *Of Woman Born*. London: Virago, 1977.

Rodgers, Bruce, *Queen's Vernacular: A Gay Lexicon*. London: Blond & Briggs, 1973.

Ross, J. M., 'Fathering: A Review of Some Psychoanalytic Contributions on Paternity', *International Journal of Psychoanalysis*, 60, (1979) 317.

Rossman, Parker, *Sexual Experience Between Men and Boys*. London: Maurice Temple Smith, 1979.

Rowse, A. L., *Homosexuals in History*. London; Weidenfeld & Nicolson, 1977.

Seabrook, Jeremy, *A Lasting Relationship: Homosexuals and Society*. London: Allen Lane, 1976.

Shipp, E. R., 'A Lesbian Who Won A Child Custody Battle', *New York Times*, 5 September 1980.

Socarides, Charles, *The Overt Homosexual*. New York: Grune & Stratton, 1968.

Standeford, W. S., 'The Bonds and Bondage of Wedlock', *The Advocate*, 23 August 1978.

Steinem, Gloria, 'Notes on the New Marriage', *New York Magazine*, 8 July 1968.

Stone, Lawrence, *The Family, Sex and Marriage in England, 1500–1800*. London: Weidenfeld & Nicolson, 1977.

Sturgis, E. T. and Admas, H. E., 'The Right to Treatment: Issues in the Treatment of Homosexuality', *Journal of Consulting and Clinical Psychology*, 46 (1978): 165–69.

Tobin, William J., *Homosexuality and Marriage; A Canonical Evaluation of the Relationship of Homosexuality to the Validity of Marriage in the Light of Recent Total Jurisprudence*. Rome: Catholic Book Agency, 1964.

Toffler, Alvin, *Future Shock*. London: Bodley Head, 1970.

Tripp, C. A., *The Homosexual Matrix*. London: Quartet, 1977.

US Department of Commerce, *American Families and Living Arrangements*. Washington: US Government Printing Office, 1980.

Vecsey, George, 'Approval Given for Homosexual to Adopt a Boy', *New York Times*, 21 June 1979.

Voeller, Bruce and Walters, James, 'Gay Fathers', *The Family Coordinator*, April 1978.

Waugh, Evelyn, *Letters*, ed. Mark Amory. London: Weidenfeld & Nicolson, 1980.

Weeks, Jeffrey, *Coming Out*. London: Quartet, 1977.

Weinberg, Martin S. and Williams, Colin J., *Male Homosexuals*. New York: Oxford University Press, 1974.

Weinstein, Allen, *Perjury: The Hiss-Chambers Case*. London: Hutchinson, 1978.

Welch, Colin, 'The Manhood of the Nation', *Daily Telegraph*, 4 November 1979.

White, Theodore, *The Making of the President, 1964*. London: Jonathan Cape, 1965.

Wilde, Oscar, *Selected Letters*. New York: Harcourt Brace & World, 1962.

Williams, Emlyn, *Emlyn*. London: Bodley Head, 1973.

Williams, Tennessee, 'Two on a Party' in *Three Players of a Summer Game and Other Stories*. London: Secker & Warburg, 1960.

Winkler, Ira and Win, Ann, *Fathers and Custody*. New York: Hawthorne Press, 1977.

Winsten, Stephen, *Salt and His Circle*. London: Hutchinson, 1951.

Woolf, Charlotte, *Bisexuality*. London: Quartet, 1977.

Index

207